GLEANINGS FROM BRITISH AND IRISH ECCLESIASTICAL HISTORY: FROM THE INTRODUCTION OF CHRISTIANITY TO THE PERIOD OF THE REFORMATION

Published @ 2017 Trieste Publishing Pty Ltd

ISBN 9780649594177

Gleanings from British and Irish Ecclesiastical History: From the Introduction of Christianity to the Period of the Reformation by Barbara Bedford

Except for use in any review, the reproduction or utilisation of this work in whole or in part in any form by any electronic, mechanical or other means, now known or hereafter invented, including xerography, photocopying and recording, or in any information storage or retrieval system, is forbidden without the permission of the publisher, Trieste Publishing Pty Ltd, PO Box 1576 Collingwood, Victoria 3066 Australia.

All rights reserved.

Edited by Trieste Publishing Pty Ltd.
Cover @ 2017

This book is sold subject to the condition that it shall not, by way of trade or otherwise, be lent, re-sold, hired out, or otherwise circulated without the publisher's prior consent in any form or binding or cover other than that in which it is published and without a similar condition including this condition being imposed on the subsequent purchaser.

www.triestepublishing.com

BARBARA BEDFORD

GLEANINGS FROM BRITISH AND IRISH ECCLESIASTICAL HISTORY: FROM THE INTRODUCTION OF CHRISTIANITY TO THE PERIOD OF THE REFORMATION

PREFACE.

THE "Gleanings from British and Irish Ecclesiastical History" now offered to the public, were first gathered up by the writer as a mental solace during lengthened periods of severe affliction and beguiled hope. As time has passed away, with regret has she observed, that a marked and unaccountable ignorance prevailed amongst otherwise well-informed persons in matters connected with the early Church history of England and our sister Island. In the hope, therefore, of engaging the attention of the generation progressing into active life to a more enlarged consideration of the subject, she has determined, although with the hesitating and enfeebled hand attendant on impaired health and declining years, to scatter her Ecclesiastical Gleanings further than she at first intended. The title she affixes to this volume at once explains its character and its limited pretensions, for history of this date cannot be expected to afford any really original matter. The writer's aim has been merely to select from the best authors those facts which it seemed desirable for every well-educated female, or intelligent person, of the middle classes, to be conversant with; but which being hardly reverted to in the pages of our national history, are only to be found fully detailed in volumes rarely within their reach; she shuns not, therefore, to avow, nay, rather feels the more confidence from acknowledging, that every event or fact recorded in the following pages has been extracted by herself from authors of the most established credit. The arrangement of them, and the connecting link of ideas, with occasional remarks thereon, are all she can claim as the genuine produce of her own pen. The Reformation in England has been so judiciously handled, by its history being adapted by the most efficient writers to the capacity of every description of reader, that she has not trespassed on that rich harvest-field of England's Church. Her only object has been to make the path thereto clearer and more fully known, and thereby more interesting and instructive; and by not only proving the existence both here and in Ireland of a Christian Church from an apostolic date, but by likewise exposing the insidious intrusions and progress of error, to warn the reader against the same quicksands, and further lead him to the conviction that the hand of Jehovah ever protected and guided to its destined purpose every event and judgment which befel these early Christian Churches. And now, at the last moment of sending this little volume forth to wend its way amongst the public, earnestly does the writer pray the blessing of the Most High may accompany it whithersoever it wanders, and that whatever may have been written amiss by man may be forgotten, and by the Lord forgiven. And if aught of benefit arise to any reader, to the Lord alone would she desire to ascribe all the might, all the power, and all the praise.

B. B.

November 12*th*, 1849.

CONTENTS.

CHAPTER I.

Introduction.—The Patriarchal and Druidical Belief, and Rites of the Primitive Britons 1

CHAPTER II.

Julius Cæsar's Invasion of Britain.—Introduction of Christianity considered.—Remarks on the word Church.—Lucius . . 10

CHAPTER III.

Ireland—By whom the Christian Religion was introduced therein.—Proofs of same.—Protestantism.—Explanation of that word . 22

CHAPTER IV.

State of Christianity in Britain after the Death of Lucius, till the Diocletian persecution.—Martyrdom of Alban.—Constantine the Great ascends the Imperial Throne.—Character of the Church universal at that time.—Council of Arles . . 29

CHAPTER V.

State of the Church during the reign of Constantine the Great.—Remarks thereon.—Pelagian Heresy.—Ireland . . . 38

CHAPTER VI.

Christian Biography.—St. Patrick.—Ireland.—Spiritual Condition of the British Church at conclusion of the Fifth Century . 46

CHAPTER VII.

Departure of Roman Legions.—Picts and Scots.—Vortigern.—Arrival and struggles with Angles and Saxons.—Biographical sketches of distinguished Christians.—Dubricius, David, Culdees, Columba, Irish Missionaries 56

CHAPTER VIII.

Bertha, the Christian Queen of the Anglo-Saxons.—Arrival of Augustine from Rome—Partial conversion of the Anglo-Saxons to Christianity, and injudicious method of extending the Christian worship amongst them.—Attempt to subjugate the Ancient British Church to the See of Rome.—Celebrated Interview with Dinoth.—Slaughter of 1,200 Monks at the Battle of Bangor Orchard.—Death of Augustine and Ethelbert . . 72

CHAPTER IX.

Relapse of Anglo-Saxons to Paganism.—Laurentius.—Eadbald.—Conversion of Edwin and his followers in Northumbria to Christianity by Paulinus.—Subsequent relapse to Paganism.—Northumbria finally converted by Aiden and Finan.—Coleman.—Wilfrid.—Council of Whitby.—Theodore . . 88

CHAPTER X.

Wilfrid's turbulent Life.—Christian Biography.—Irish and British Missionaries on the Continent.—Aldhelm.—Bede.—Alcuin . 105

CHAPTER XI.

Irish Missionaries.—Ina.—Peter's Pence.—Offa.—Egbert, sole King of England.—Ethelwolf.—Alfred.—Danish Invaders subjected to Church rates, &c.—Athelstan.—Erection of Churches.—Dunstan; Introduction of Benedictine Monks.—Ethelred.—Canute.—Elfrid.—William the Conqueror . . . 116

CHAPTER XII.

William the Conqueror.—Alterations in Church matters.—Romish intrigues respecting the Irish Church.—William Rufus—Anselm.—Contentions and encroachments on the Liberty of both English and Irish Churches continued during the time of Henry I., when the Primitive British Church merged into the Anglo-Saxon.—Continued resistance of the Irish Church to Romish Aggression.—Grant of Ireland by Adrian to Henry II. . 135

CHAPTER XIII.

Henry II. invades and proclaims himself King of Ireland.—Heretics first condemned as such at Oxford.—Thomas-à-Becket.—Crusades.—John.—State of Church in Ireland.—Robert Grossetête, Bishop of Lincoln.—Dominicans and Franciscans introduced into England.—Henry III.—Remarks on Ireland 149

CHAPTER XIV.

Edward I.—Ireland.—Edward II.—The distinctive marks of two Irish Churches at that time.—Edward III.—Bradwardine.—Edward's efforts to retard the encroachments of the Popish Clergy.—Partially successful in England.—Nullified in Ireland through their intrigues procuring the enactment of the Statutes of Kilkenny 161

CHAPTER XV.

Wickliff.—State of the Clergy in England.—Lollards.—Henry IV.—His Policy.—Arundel.—Lord Cobham.—Public Commotions.—Reynold Pecock, Bishop of Chichester.—Art of Printing introduced into England 174

CHAPTER XVI.

Remarks on the reign of Henry VII.—Rebellion in Ireland, and the nature of a Romish Oath.—Henry VIII. ascends the

Throne of England.—Disputes with the Pope.—Shakes off the Supremacy of the Pope.—Persecutions.—Suppression of Monasteries, &c., &c., &c.—Bad Policy respecting Ireland . 187

CHAPTER XVII.

Observations on Destruction of Monasteries.—Pope excommunicates and denounces Henry.—Bible translated.—Romish Policy towards Henry.—Consequent death of Cromwel.—Act of Six Articles passed.—King's Book published.—Persecutions arising therefrom.—Machinations of the Romish party, and Martyrdoms of Protestants alluded to.—Death of Henry.—His character.—General Observations, and Conclusion . 211

APPENDIX.

No. I.
General Observations on the word Protestant . . . 229

No. II.
General Observations on Liturgies 231

No. III.
Bibles 233

No. IV.
Canons 235

No. V.
Concluding Remarks on the progress of the Reformation in Ireland 235

GLEANINGS FROM BRITISH AND IRISH ECCLESIASTICAL HISTORY.

CHAPTER I.

Introduction.—The Patriarchal and Druidical Belief, and Rites of the Primitive Britons.

AMIDST the waste waters of oblivion, o'er which the prying historian is wont to cast an anxious glance, the Holy Scriptures alone offer him a footing from whence he may catch the first glimpse of past events, as they emerge from off its dark and obscured surface, and, entering on the stream of time, successively approach our era,—that stream which now holds encircled in its eddy the present generation of man, and is likewise propelling it onward, with hurried force, to launch it into the unfathomable depths of eternity.

The truth of this introductory remark will be unequivocally established by the immediate appeal we must have to Sacred Writ, in the very few remarks which it seems desirable to make (in connexion with the early Church History of Britain) respecting its first inhabitants; from whom they sprang; from whence they came; and what religious knowledge they brought with them.

The earliest records that have reached us on this subject are found in the Welsh Triads. These interesting relics of traditional history, in their narration of the peopling of this island, make mention of a mythical personage, named Hu Gradran, or, Hu the Mighty, as having led the Kymry, or Cymry (which signifies the first race), from Defrobani (or the summer country),* to this island. Alluding also to the Deluge, the Ark, and the plains of Shinar, it is impossible not to identify this Hu with Noah. The more accredited detail of Herodotus seems so much to strengthen this national and bardic representation of events, that historians generally allow that this island must have been peopled by the Cymry, who are the acknowledged descendants of Ashkenaz, the eldest son of Gomer, the eldest son of Japhet, the eldest son of Noah. The scriptural confirmation of this idea is found in the tenth chapter of Genesis, fifth verse: "By these were the isles of the Gentiles divided in their lands; every one after his tongue, after their families, in their nations." There can be no doubt that the religion which, by the appointment of God, had been the means of salvation to many† of the Antediluvian patriarchs, was preserved and taught by Noah to his children, and also among some of his posterity, for many generations after the deluge. Whilst the recollection of that tremendous judgment was fresh and powerful in the minds of men, they probably adhered thereto, and diligently taught their children the same.

The following leading points, therefore, of their patriarchal religion, were probably preserved amongst the Celts and Cymry:—A clear and distinct knowledge

---

* Where Constantinople now stands.
† Heb. xi. 5—7. Abel, Enoch, Noah.

of the one true and living God, as the Creator of the universe, and man's responsibility to him, in all things, as his rightful Lord and moral Governor;—the history, also, of man's fall by the temptation of the devil, by which was established the existence of fallen angels, and man's constant liability to their assaults and temptations;—the appointment of one day in seven as a day of rest, to be devoted to religious pursuits;—a definite idea of good and evil, or what is meant by "doing well, and not doing well," and the legitimate and inevitable consequences of each;—a distinct apprehension of the immortality of the *soul* in a future state of existence, and of the last judgment. Withal, a believing expectation of the great Deliverer, promised to man under the distinguished name of "the seed of the woman," whose work was at the same time defined to be, the bruising of the serpent's head, or destroying the power of Satan. And further, the offering of sacrifices at stated times,* to represent the demerit of sin, that men might be excited to repentance; and to typify the death by which that promised Deliverer should atone for sin, that thereby man might constantly be reminded of Him in whom they should trust for salvation, and exercise faith.†

With such a religious knowledge and belief, and its corresponding benefits, we may therefore presume the Cymry (as one of the Celtic tribes and acknowledged descendants of Ashkenaz) arrived here, and first imprinted the sand on Albion's shores with the foot of man.

Besides the benefits accruing from such a knowledge of God, and his worship and fear, their proper share of

* Gen. viii. 20. "And Noah builded an altar unto the Lord."
† Abel, Enoch, Noah. Heb. xi. 4, 5, 7.

Noah's prophetic blessing* likewise accompanied the descendants of Japhet in their migration from the East across the Continent of Europe. However, clear it is that the highest honour was then reserved for Shem, the second son of Noah, namely, that from amongst them Abram should be called to become the father of the chosen family and nation, by whom the true worship of God was to be preserved, and from amongst whom the Deliverer, the Messiah, was to appear; ere the Japhethites (by whom the isles of the Gentiles were to be peopled) † left the patriarchal hive, their participation also in the afore-stated expected blessing (and in which as the fallen offspring of Adam they were so deeply interested) was genealogically secured to them. ‡

In the prophetic announcement just referred to, of the selection of the Hebrews as the chosen people of God, and which, for a time, was alone revealed to them, for "unto the descendants of Eber were the oracles of God committed," great care, it may be observed, was taken to remind the favoured race to whose custody those prophetic blessings were to be so exclusively intrusted, that they were the younger brethren of the Japhethites.

[B.C. 2347.] Though the Japhethites were then departing, somewhat like the prodigal son, and going "into a far country," their brotherhood was not to be cut off for ever. The time was foreknown, in the counsel of the Most High, when, through the preaching of the apostles, the prodigal son was to come to himself, and

* Gen. ix. 27. "God shall enlarge (or persuade) Japhet, and he shall dwell in the tents of Shem."
† Gen. x. 5.
‡ Gen. x. 21. "Unto Shem also, the father of all the children of Eber, the brother of Japhet the elder."

they who were aliens from the promises were to be made fellow-citizens with the household of God, and return to seek their Father's face. In the twenty-seventh verse of the ninth chapter of Genesis, we find the special assurance to Japhet implied, that God should enlarge (or *persuade*, margin) him, a term that seems to convey the idea of spiritual, as well as temporal, blessing and expansion. All history bears witness to the fulfilment of this prophecy, and that this country has pre-eminently shared in these promised gifts; for has not Britain's earthly portion enlarged much beyond its original limits, and have not multitudes of its possessors enjoyed the blessing of enlarged or persuaded hearts and minds?

Though the information which can be obtained from the Welsh triads and other sources, respecting the social habits and religious belief and worship of the earliest inhabitants of Britain, is very imperfect, sufficient has been gathered by the learned investigators of them to satisfy humbler inquirers that they each bore a patriarchal character. Their worship must sensibly have approached that professed and practised by the Hebrew patriarchs before their departure into Egypt, or the giving of the Law at Mount Sinai. Like them, the head of each family conducted the religious services of the social circle, and offered the required sacrifices. The first departure of the Britons from the simplicity of the worship of their progenitors, appeared in their appointment of particular individuals into a distinct class, to establish a regular priesthood. When this step took place is not known, but its adoption is attributed by writers to the influence and example of heathen traders from the East. At the earliest period of its existence, Druidical belief has thus been described:—" Though there was manifested in the worship of the Druids a singular combination of the worship of many gods (the leading ones bearing the names of Thau, Hesus, &c.), it does not appear to have interfered with, or superseded, an acknowledged recognition of belief in an only 'one God,' who, they confessed, was the one source of life, and sole giver of good. His duration they defined as eternal, and omnipotence the measure of his power. Amongst their names for this 'one supreme God' are terms which have been translated God, Distributor, Governor, The Mysterious One, The Eternal, The Ancient of Days, and to him, their 'only God,' does it seem they ascribed government, or providence, or offered the genuine essence of their worship or sacrifices. The only objects of their further veneration were the wildest and sublimest objects of nature. They had no idols, justly considering that the Divine Power could be adored unseen. Like the Hebrew patriarchs, they worshipped in the open air, their favourite place being a grove,* or the shelter of some majestic tree, such as the oak,† and they held nothing so sacred as the mistletoe, and the tree on which it was produced, provided it were an oak."

They called the mistletoe by a name which, in their language, signified the curer of all ills. In the foregoing, and in further particulars, may be traced the traditional remembrance which had been handed down to them of the Almighty God and the promised

---

* "Abraham planted a grove in Beersheba, and called there on the name of the Lord, the everlasting God." (Gen. xxi. 33.)

† Jacob buried his dead "beneath Bethel, under an oak." (Gen. xxxv. 8.) And Joshua "took a great stone, and set it up under an oak that was by the sanctuary of the Lord." (Joshua xxiv. 26.)

Saviour. In proceeding with the history of the British Church, we shall not find that Druidism is a solitary proof of the evil tendency of tradition in matters of religious belief, or its rites. It will, therefore, be useful to keep our eye fixed on its influence from this early date, and mark, through succeeding ages to the present time, the numerous evidences, as they appear in ecclesiastical history, of the crumbling and perishable nature of its materials.

The Druids, in their more sacred spots, erected also stone pillars,* placing them in circular rows; thus again exhibiting the distinctive features of their patriarchal origin. Some remains of these temples of our forefathers still exist. They believed likewise in the immortality of the soul. At the period referred to, the Britons were celebrated for their religious knowledge and zeal. As a people, they were neither ignorant nor careless; they knew the principles of their faith, and diligently attended to it and the counsels of their priests and instructors—the Druids. The remote and insular situation of Britain, for many centuries, preserved the worship of its inhabitants purer than that of any other Pagan country. It must, however, have gradually yielded to the evil influence of the Phœnicians, Egyptians, and Grecians, who visited Cornwall and other parts, in search of tin and other metals, and who accordingly left the impress of their respective idolatrous beliefs and practices behind them, tending to all that was vitiated and bad; for we

* See the entire account of Jacob's conduct at Bethel (Gen. xxviii. 18, 19), and observe the similar conduct of Moses: "And Moses rose up early in the morning, and builded an altar under the hill, and twelve pillars, according to the twelve tribes of Israel." (Exod. xxiv. 4.)

find that heathenish ceremonies were subsequently performed in honour of Baal, or Bel, &c., &c. Resort was then had to high places,* and the fires that flamed to his honour in such situations, on the 1st of April, were called the Bealtine.

[B.C. 600.] Hercules was also worshipped in Britain, at a still later date, under the name of Ogmius. Though from henceforward we also find the increasing mention of other heathen deities, in connexion with Druidical worship, it must not be taken for granted that they entirely adopted the mythology of those gods. Heathen writers, it seems clear, mention the subject more in conformity with their own ideas of those gods, than such as were truly entertained by the Druids; for it is evident that they never sank into the polytheism of Greece and Rome. Though the patriarchal religion is thus exhibited, as gradually and lamentably becoming more and more debased, from the period when the simplicity of Druidical worship (from resting only on tradition) first yielded to the influence of heathenish practices introduced from the East,—it was not entirely corrupted till the Romans, being also attracted to Britain, engrafted on them their still darker mythology.

[B.C. 55.] Then, indeed, may it be said the Britons sat down in darkness and the shadow of death. Their spiritual renovation, however, was not unprovided for, nor very far distant; for fifty-five years after Cæsar's ambition had aspiringly induced him to attempt the subjugation of "the sea-girt island," "the Day-spring

---

* "And the lords of the high places of Arnon." (Numb. xxi. 28.) "And Balak took Balaam, and brought him up into the high places of Baal." (Numb. xxii. 4.)

from on high" had arisen; and the plains of Bethlehem had resounded with the joyous anthem of the heavenly host, proclaiming to the whole fallen race of man, whether Jew or Gentile, that the Messiah, their Redeemer, had appeared on earth.

The Lord Jesus, having fulfilled all righteousness, at length suffered, and died, and rose again; but ere he re-ascended to his Father's throne, he commissioned his apostles to "go into the world, and preach the Gospel to every creature." (Matthew xxviii. 19; Mark xvi. 15.)

CHAPTER II.

Julius Cæsar's Invasion of Britain.—Introduction of Christianity considered.—Remarks on the word Church.—Lucius.

[B. C. 55.] WE find no difficulty in ascertaining the spot, the year, the month, the day, and the hour, when Cæsar, for the gratification of his insatiable ambition, left the coast of Gaul to attempt the conquest of Britain,* and first defiled its fair surface with the shadow of a foreign foe; and if possessed of the power of foreknowledge, Satan doubtless rejoiced;† for, as the golden eagle banner of Pagan Rome was unfurled, and he first beheld it flutter to a British breeze, he must have recognised the ensign of Papal Rome, under whose mysterious agency he might hope, when the banner of the cross waved throughout the land, to be enabled to beguile and retain unto himself a people from amongst the inhabitants of Christianized Britain.

Can we, however, in behalf of the subject of our research, or, as haply amongst the number of those who have been awakened to a conviction of the value

---

* He set sail from Portus Itius, between Calais and Boulogne, at ten o'clock on the morning of August 26th, 55 B.C. He landed on Albion's shore on a spot between Walmer Castle and Sandwich.

† 1 Kings xxiii. 22: "I will go forth, and be a lying spirit in the mouth of all his prophets," &c. Job i., ii.; Luke xxii. 31: "Satan hath desired to have you, that he may sift you as wheat." Matt. viii. 29: "What have we to do with thee, Jesus, thou Son of God? Art thou come hither to torment us before the time?"

of an immortal soul, and the costly price paid for its redemption, learn the spot where the first Briton knelt to the Lord Jehovah? Can we trace his name? or can we surmise when Satan trembled for his future sovereignty in this land, when the first repentant Briton supplicating cried, " Father, I have sinned against heaven and before thee, and am no more worthy to be called thy son," and further beheld the gracious Father go forth to meet and welcome the long-lost Japhethite? Who has ventured to identify the honoured servant whom the Father called from amongst his household of faith to bring forth the best robe, (the imputed righteousness of Christ,) and bid him array in that spotless garment the prodigal Gentile, who, standing in his fur-adorned, yet half-clad state, gathered up the words of life as they fell from his lips? Involving the eternal interests of each succeeding generation of Britons, it is unquestionably the most important event that has ever taken place in our fatherland.

With wearied disappointment, however, are the pages of history turned over for information on that subject. All, to our research, seems lost and sunk in oblivion. But is it so? No! from sacred writ we learn that the name of the first repentant Briton whom the shining ranks of angels, in the presence of God rejoiced over, is safely enrolled amongst the Church of the first-born, and his name written in the book of life,—so written, that, when the Lord Jesus, who claimed him of the Father as the first-fruits of his inheritance from " the uttermost parts of the earth," (Ps. ii.), "cometh with tens of thousands of his saints, to execute judgment on all," (Jude 14, 15,) "then shall he also appear with him in glory." (Col. iii. 4.)

The general outlines of recorded facts satisfactorily

prove, that the introduction of Christianity must be attributed to the circumstance of the brave and kingly Caractacus being taken prisoner by the Romans while defending his country from their intrusion, and being led a captive, with some others of his family, to Rome. The overruling power and will of the Most High had destined the propitious hour when they should arrive there, for there also lay in bonds St. Paul, the great Apostle of the Gentiles; and with him, it appears, this captive and distinguished family formed a friendship, the result being the conversion of Bran, the father of Caractacus, and likewise that of his daughter, Claudia, to the Christian faith.

Her name, and that it is presumed, of her Roman husband, Rufus, (Rom. xvi. 13,) otherwise mentioned as Pudens, are honoured by being named in Scripture. (2 Tim. iv. 21.) Doubts have been raised by some writers as to the identity of Claudia; but every circumstance having been investigated by the learned, the same are now little regarded.*

[A.D. 58.] The family of Caractacus was detained

---

* Perhaps it may interest the young reader to have placed before him an epigram of Martial, one of the Roman poets, in confirmation of the identity of Claudia.

Before her marriage it runs thus:—

"From painted Britons how was Claudia born?
The fair barbarian! how do arts adorn!
When Roman charms, a Grecian soul commend,
Athens and Rome may for the dame contend."

After her marriage with Pudens, he thus writes:—

"Oh, Rufus! Pudens, whom I own my friend,
Has ta'en the foreign Claudia for his wife.
Propitious Hymen, light thy torch and send
Long years of bliss to their united life."

seven years at Rome, during the two last of which St. Paul was a prisoner at large in that city, and they were all released from their captivity therein at the same time. The best accredited authorities suppose that in St. Paul's liberation from this, his first captivity, and during his eight years' absence from Rome, he accompanied Bran, and other British converts, to their native land, and that he preached the Gospel there. Through the instrumentality, therefore, of this already distinguished and enlightened family, it is conjectured, the name of Jesus was so early heard in this distant region, accomplishing thereby one of our Lord's own predictions: that before the fall of Jerusalem the Gospel should be preached throughout the whole world. (Matt. xxiv. 14; Mark xiii. 30.) Britain then formed the extremity of the known world. Many historians and writers express their belief that St. Paul founded a Christian Church in Britain; and, before he left it, ordained Aristobulus—mentioned in the 16th chapter of his Epistle to the Romans, and 10th verse—the first bishop. Aristobulus, it is also said, finally died a martyr in the cause of Christ by the hands of the Pagan natives. At this first mention of the word Church it may be well to inquire into its original, spiritual, and truest meaning; and as the Bible is the text-book of the Church of England, (whose history we are gathering,) we will turn to its sacred pages for the information we desire. We accordingly find the word Church is first used by the great Head of the Church, the Lord Jesus, in reference to his being the Rock on which he would build his Church, "and on this rock I will build my Church." (Matt. xvi. 18.) In 1 Cor. i. 2, St. Paul describes the Church as an assembly selected and called out of the world by the doctrine of the Gospel, to the worship of the true God in Christ, according to his word. Observe, not according to the traditions or words of any man, but only according to the Word of God. In the first chapter of St. Paul's Epistle to the Colossians, he clearly represents it as an assemblage of saints and faithful brethren, from the beginning to the end of the world, who make but one body, whereof Jesus Christ is the Head. The faithful also of one family who assembled with other Christians to worship with them at their house he styles, "the Church." (Romans xvi. 5.) "Greet the Church that is in their house." Again, (Col. iv. 15,) "Salute the brethren which are at Laodicea, and Nymphas, and the Church which is in his house." In Philemon, the second verse, greeting him and other faithful Christians, he adds,— "And Archippus our fellow-soldier, and to the Church in thy house." The faithful, also, in some one province he acknowledges as the Church; for in 2 Thess. i. 1, we read, "unto the Church of the Thessalonians."

In Matt. xviii. 17, we find it applied by the Lord himself to the governors, or representatives of the Church: "Tell it to the Church;" that is, to such rulers to whom the censures of the Church do of right belong; that by them it may be communicated to the whole body. It is thus clearly demonstrated to be a scriptural term, applied only to true believers. Ever since the apostolic age it has, nevertheless, been subject to the misapplication of the ignorant, and the presumptuous assumptions of false professors, for the purpose of furthering their own intriguing motives and designs.

In returning to the immediate subject of these pages, we must observe, that, however interesting it may be, to connect the great Apostle of the Gentiles with the introduction of Christianity into our fatherland, it must be borne in mind, that the evidence respecting it, is more drawn from inference than from positive demonstration. It is, however, clearly proved that the blessed light of the Gospel of peace shone here so early and so clearly, that a Christian Church was undoubtedly, established here during the apostolic age. We know not, indeed, who enkindled the radiant spark; but this we know, that all the machinations of Satan, the great enemy of souls, to extinguish it have not prevailed; and that it still burns as the national beacon of Christian safety to our native land.

With reverence would we here remark, that the Almighty, foreknowing the future abominations which would settle round the names and memories of distinguished and pious individuals, may (in mercy to succeeding generations) purposely have so cast the veil of uncertainty over the subject under consideration as to obscure it; and thus has baffled the baneful consequences of superstitious and monkish veneration, which might have attended clearer evidence on the subject.

Besides the already mentioned Claudia, another British female of distinction, Pomponia Græcina, the wife of Aulus Plautius, the first Roman Governor of Britain, we are informed, also embraced Christianity. Ultimately she passed many melancholy years on account of her Christian belief and faith in Pagan Rome. In addition to that of St. Paul, several other scriptural names have been mentioned in connexion with the evangelizing of the Britons. Some monkish writers, of Norman date, state that Joseph of Arimathea was despatched by Philip from Gaul, being accompanied by twelve companions, amongst whom they enumerate Lazarus, Martha, and Mary Magdalene, with Marcella, their servant, and that they were allowed to fix themselves at Glastonbury, then ordinarily called the Isle of Avalon, or Isle of Apples. Against this relation, long supported by every assistance that such writers could give it, (from tales of miracles and other marvels), such grave objections arise, that the whole is looked on as a fabrication. The British name, Yrys, vitrym, the glassy isle, had been, perhaps, given to it as descriptive of the locality, which was then composed of watery marshes, surrounded with sluggish streams. Druidism had, probably, left therein a residence hallowed by a supposed sanctity, which the Christian teachers imagined would render their labours more acceptable to the neighbouring population. This is most likely the true history of the sacred character which Glastonbury acquired in her early days. On the Saxon invasion, her water-locked recesses, in a remote part of the country, would naturally offer a suitable shelter for a congregation of British Christians escaping from pursuit and persecution, and perhaps the wattled Church of their construction, at a subsequent period, might eventually have been appropriated by those invaders to their own use, when converted to Christianity. If this ancient place of worship had been supposed to possess pretensions of a character yet more illustrious, it is by no means likely that the same would have been overlooked by Gildas, the British, as well as the most ancient and truest of historians; either by Bede, the Saxon Romanist, or any of the other writers who succeeded him prior to the Norman conquest. No mention being made of Joseph of Arimathea, and Glastonbury, previous to that event, it is evident that the sanctity with which the place had been previously invested, was seized upon by the monkish writers, after the Norman conquest, as a likely medium for assisting and supporting their legendary and superstitious tales respecting saints and relics. Their fabulous traditions are further repudiated by the statement they set forth, that the Church, built there by Joseph and his followers, was dedicated to the Virgin Mary; nowhere is mention made of the dedication of churches to any of the saints, in the first century. They further state, that he was buried within its precincts; whereas no burial within such buildings, or even in church-yards, was known till the time of Cuthbert, Archbishop of Canterbury, who died A.D. 798.

Though very little is known of the actual progress of Christianity during this period in Britain, there can be no doubt, that the worship of its followers accorded with the general practice of the primitive Eastern Churches; a brief sketch of which may not be inappropriate at this point of our inquiries. Individuals who had been convinced of sin by the preaching of the Gospel, had humbled themselves in penitential sorrow, and sought deliverance by earnest prayer, and found redemption from their sin by simple faith in Christ, formed the members of a Christian Church. As their numbers increased, it called forth the necessity of appointing regular pastors to each Church. We are informed the service was conducted in the following order:—First, the holy Scriptures were read; then, psalms or hymns were sung; afterwards, the sermon was preached by the Bishop or Presbyter, which, generally, was an explanation of the lessons; and the devotion was concluded by solemn prayer.

In this manner, there can be no doubt, the religion

of Christ was publicly professed and disseminated in Britain. It encountered and subdued, through the gracious influence of the Holy Spirit working with it, the native superstition of the island; it overcame the more polished and abominable heathenism that had been imported from Rome; and had done so much towards spreading a knowledge of the Christian doctrine, and offering the salvation of the Gospel unto its benighted inhabitants, that when Lucius [A.D. 176] (who is represented as the third in descent from Caractacus) assumed the sovereignty, numbers of the natives were ready to unite with him in his efforts for firmly establishing it.* Lucius, indeed, proved himself a nursing father to this infant Christian Church, which, ever since the Apostolic age, had been struggling unprotected amidst the Paganism of Britain. For the purpose of obtaining further information he despatched ambassadors to Rome. It is certain that Lucius divided the kingdom into several ecclesiastical districts, appointing bishops to various leading localities. The first he founded were those of Llandaff and Caerleon; and they must ever be borne in recollection, with peculiar interest, as the sees of the greatest antiquity, and as a proof that Christianity had been generally received by the pristine tribes, over whom this kingly individual ruled. Caerleon had other names affixed to it when it became a Roman station. The Romans, it seems, invariably gave an additional name to a city or place they dignified as a colony, and favoured with a governor. The see of Caerleon is consequently

* He is also spoken of in ancient records under the name of "Llewrwy," or "Lleufu Mawr," or "the great luminary," probably bestowed upon him in consideration of his having promoted the cause of Christianity.

often mentioned under the appellation of " Urbs Legiones," likewise of "Isca Legio Secunda Augusta."* The see of Llandaff, with that of Caerleon, and the later one of St. David's (Menapia, or Menavia) often merged one into the other, from being respectively held by the same individuals, and consequently it has led to much confusion in the details of the ecclesiastical history of that Principality; but it has also led to the clear demonstration of the thorough independence of the ancient British Church, for, when the Romish had obtained a footing in England, if it had been subject to that see, (even as late as the twelfth century,) on the appeal by Giraldis Cambrensis to that power, an appointment from the Pope would have settled the question then at issue.

In the New Testament, the terms Presbyter and Bishop are indifferently applied to the same office, in the Church, as being overseers of the Christian flocks intrusted to their particular care. The early Bishops of this island (as well as elsewhere) are represented to us as having been strictly primitive in their habits, as well as in their ideas, respecting dignity or ecclesiastical power.

Besides the two earliest bishoprics of Llandaff and Caerleon, which Lucius is described as having founded, it is asserted that he added several others in different parts of the island,—some authors state as many as twenty-eight.

To Lucius, also, is attributed the conversion of many Pagan temples into Christian Churches, especially that of Diana, on which site now stands St. Paul's, London; and that consecrated to Apollo, now Westminster

* From the British " Wysg," a current, course, or stream.

Abbey; St. Peter's, also, Cornhill, was the seat of the first Bishop of London (Theanus), which bishopric was also founded by Lucius. It is affirmed that he built St. Martin's Church, near Canterbury, which afterwards was appropriated to the service of Bertha, the Christian consort of the Saxon pagan king, Ethelwald. The erection of churches at Glastonbury, Bangor, and Winchester is ascribed to him. As the first ruling power who acknowledged and professed the Christian faith, not only in Britain, but, it is presumed, in Europe also, we yet can trace the fact that, under the sway of Lucius, the ancient privileges enjoyed by the Druids were transferred to the Christians. The triads describe Lucius as "one of the blessed princes of the isle of Britain, who built the first church of Llandav, which was the first in the isle of Britain, and who gave the privilege of the country and the tribe, with civil and ecclesiastical rights, to those who possessed faith in Christ."

The different immunities, to which the Druids as national ministers of religion and teachers of the arts had been entitled, were the following:—Five free acres of land; exemption from personal attendance in war; permission to pass unmolested from one district to another, in time of war as well as in peace; exemption from land-tax; and a contribution from every plough in the district in which they were the authorized teachers." The legal transference of these to the Christian priesthood formed one of the leading features of Lucius's political regulations.

Though the testimonies which have been handed down to us respecting this kingly individual vary as to the extent of his dominions, and the precise date when he effected these changes, the benefits he conferred on the British Church must, undoubtedly, have been very great. These facts have also reached us free from the palpable and extravagant embellishments of miracles, and undue reverence for saints, and of submission and subjection to Rome, found so abundantly in the monkish histories respecting earlier ages written at a later date, to suit their own views and purposes. Yet has the history of Lucius not entirely escaped; for the mission he sent to Rome, seeking information on Roman jurisprudence, has been unworthily seized on by them, whereon to base, and send forth to after ages, an unfounded insinuation that his conversion to Christianity was attributable to Romish instruction and influence. The reply of the Bishop Eleutherius to Lucius, and which is supposed to be the most ancient writing extant relative to the Christian religion in England, presents a totally different aspect; and, moreover, establishes the thorough independent character of the British Church; for Eleutherius twice calls King Lucius, "God's vicar in his kingdom."

CHAPTER III.

*Ireland—By whom the Christian Religion was introduced therein.
—Proofs of same.—Protestantism.—Explanation of that Word.*

WE must now direct our attention to the religious state of our sister island during the two first centuries. In doing so, it is of importance to state (and to remember also) that the name Scotia (or Scotland), as applicable to the northern portion of Britain, is comparatively of modern origin. The primitive Scots were that branch of the great Celtic nation, who, at a period beyond all authentic history, had established themselves in Hibernia, or Erin, now Ireland. Hence that island, by the writers of the sixth or seventh century, is generally called Scotia, or Insular Scotorum; and, by the consent of all antiquity, the name of Scoti belonged to the Irish alone till the eleventh century. Such historians speak of Ireland as the mother of the Scots, and Caledonia as the parent of the Picts. The Picts were originally Britons, who, living beyond the Roman boundary, had maintained and continued in the enjoyment of their independence during the sojourn of the Romans in this island. Hibernia, or Ireland (like this country), probably received the knowledge of Christianity through the means of Eastern missionaries, and about the same date it is supposed,—as a Christian Church, it is allowed, was established there in the apostolic age. From the researches of the learned, it appears conclusive that the Primitive Church of Ireland was not only of eastern origin, but was derived therefrom, in an immediate line from the disciples or followers of St. John the Evangelist, or the Divine. The precise period, however, when it was originally introduced cannot now be fully ascertained; nor are we to be surprised at this, as a similar uncertainty envelops the first establishment of Christian Churches in Britain, Gaul, Spain, and Rome itself. It is granted by historians generally, that Ireland was visited by the disciples of Christ within one hundred years of the crucifixion, and through the means of Irenæus and Photinus, who were the disciples of Polycarp, and preached the Gospel with such success in Gaul; and through whose means flourishing and testifying Churches were also established in Lyons and Vienna, of which places Photinus was the first Bishop. These distinguished missionaries were the disciples of Polycarp, the disciple of Ignatius, the immediate disciple of St. John. In this line of missionaries may clearly be perceived the meaning of that memorable declaration, at a later date, of St. Coleman at the Council of Whitby (A. D. 664), respecting the celebration of Easter:—"I marvel how some men call that absurd in which we follow the example of so great an apostle,—one who was thought worthy of reposing on the bosom of his Lord; and can it be believed that such men, as our venerable father Columkill and his successors would have thought, and acted things contrary to the precepts of the sacred pages?" Again: "This Easter, which I used to observe, I received from my elders, who sent the Bishop hither, which all our fathers, beloved of God, are known to have celebrated after the same manner." And again: "It is the same which the blessed Evangelist St. John, the disciple especially beloved by our Lord, with all the Churches that he oversaw is read to have celebrated."

St. Irenæus, the Bishop of Lyons, (A.D. 100,) mentions the existence of Churches amongst the Celtic nations, but the earliest writer who affords the most direct proof of the probable existence of one in Ireland is Tertullian, one of the Latin fathers, who wrote about the year 200. He asserts, "that those parts of the British isles which were unapproached by the Romans were yet subject to Christ." The allusion to Ireland is here manifest, from the use of the plural noun. This immediate connexion of the disciples of St. John with the formation of the Christian Church in Ireland may perhaps account for the religious veneration exhibited by the Irish for the number seven. Witness the celebrated seven churches, evidently selected in honour of him, and as an humble imitation and remembrance of the seven primitive churches of the Book of Revelation, and to whom this Apostle of the early saints of Ireland addressed his seven epistles from the isle that is called Patmos. The oft-repeated and continued efforts of Romish writers to attribute the christianizing of either Britain or Ireland to Romish missionaries is thus, by the preceding brief sketch, extracted from the soundest and most trustworthy author of the present age, completely refuted. May the little which has been extracted from their learned labours, and thus laid before youthful readers, stimulate them to further research into the subject, and prevent their being led astray by such gross misrepresentations. Much may be gathered from the characteristic evidence we possess that both our native Churches, though perfectly distinct from each other, exhibited traces of a genuine eastern origin.

The simple nature of this little volume renders it only suitable to mention the most prominent of them. None can be more so than the time when each of them celebrated the festival of Easter, both of them adopting that established by the primitive Churches in the East, in direct opposition to that chosen by the Romish Church.

As respects the Irish Church, her Liturgy (the Cursus Scotorum)* was of oriental origin, having been brought from Alexandria. A further and striking proof of the Eastern, and consequently the Anti-Romish origin of the Irish Church, appears to be the great multitude of bishops in Ireland, where they were changed and increased at pleasure.†

Choriepiscopi, or village bishops, existed as an order long after they had been discontinued in the Romish Church.

The Irish, as well as the British Christians, of these early ages, received the Communion of the Lord's Supper in both kinds, calling it the Communion of the body and blood of their Lord and Saviour. The mass, a term which now might be misunderstood, and consequently misconstrued, was nothing more than that used for the public service of the Church, when only the prayers were said, without the celebration of the Communion. When the historical features of this pristine period are also taken into consideration, the Romish claim is still further nullified; for they present to our

---

* A Discourse on Liturgies, published by Spelman from a MS. upwards of 1,000 years old, happily enables the learned to ascertain its nature and contents.

† In like manner we read, that St. Basil, in the fourth century, had fifty rural bishops in his see: and that there were 500 sees in the six African provinces.

view the fact, that in the reign of Con, Ireland in the second century sent forth, as a missionary to other parts of Europe, the famous St. Cathaldus, to preach therein the blessed doctrines of Christianity. He ultimately became Bishop and patron of Tarentum, in Italy. In the next age, Cormas, an Irish prince, and a celebrated legislator, was converted to Christianity and died in the faith.

Do not the foregoing facts testify to the unprejudiced reader that evangelized Ireland received the bright beams of Gospel light from an earlier and purer ray than Papal Rome?

As succeeding pages will advance our research into her history, we shall find, on the authority of the ablest and most convincing historian* of the present day, that, like her Waldensian sister in the wilderness, she has always been a Protestant Church:—in the primitive ages, appearing as a witness against the usurped authority of Rome; and at later dates, protesting against the doctrines and practices of her corrupt system of religion.

No better place in these pages can, perhaps, be selected than the present for making a few remarks on the origin of Protestantism; for some persons affirm that it was first heard of at the time of the Lutheran Reformation, but a careful investigation of the subject will prove it was of an earlier growth. Ever since the time of the apostles' preaching the Gospel, the Church of Christ has been a protesting Church against all error and false doctrine. Did not the apostles themselves protest against the errors and Antichrists which had appeared in the very Churches they had established? For many ages after the religion of Jesus Christ was first established, the great body of Christians scattered

* Murray.

over the whole world was called the holy Catholic Church, the word catholic signifying general, or universal. The Christians having one Lord, one faith, one baptism, were agreed also in all the great articles of faith; and the congregations of different countries and kingdoms worshipped their common Saviour according to forms which were so much alike, that, though there might be some differences in point of discipline, yet, as the branches of the same stem make one tree, so they made one Church of Christ. One great reason why the primitive Christians continued fast bound together, in this communion of saints and fellowship of the holy Catholic Church, arose from nobody of any character for piety or scriptural knowledge ever attempting to introduce objects, doctrines, or services, which were opposed to the written Word of God, or the simplicity of the Gospel. Another reason was, that no universal Church endeavoured to lord it over another, or to assume the pre-eminence. There was nothing forced upon the will; there was nothing to sear the conscience, or make a devout man feel, that, by his conformity to the Church, he was acting contrary to the will of God. But when the time came (as St. Paul prophesied it should come, 2 Thess. ii. 3, 4, 9, 10, and 1 Tim. iv. 1, 3), when the seamless robe of Christ was torn, and the Church of Rome apostatized from the religion taught by Christ and his apostles; then humbler, and, in those parts, less numerous but more pious, congregations, were obliged to protest against such errors, and afterwards to separate from those who held them; and this, in the general acceptation of the word, is the origin of Protestantism.*

* See Appendix, No. 1.

The first act, in general ecclesiastical history, which comes under this name, was that of Irenæus, and of the Christians of Gaul (A.D. 200), when they protested against the tyranny and intolerance of Victor, Bishop of Rome, who endeavoured to force on them his own opinion and practices.

In our progress, we shall further learn how the melancholy change in Ireland's ecclesiastical affairs and social welfare took place, when, instead of being *in advance* of all other nations in religion and general literature, she will, ever after a given period, appear amongst them with a clouded and bewildered aspect. One design of this little volume is, to lay before the rising generation a more faithful outline of Ireland's religious history than has hitherto been generally within their reach. May it not only awaken their intellectual interest, but arouse their energies, and exhibit to them, from a faithful record of past events, their responsibilities as Protestants toward our sister land! May the Lord himself once more look on her in mercy, and say unto her, "Arise, shine, for thy light is come, and the glory of the Lord is risen upon thee." (Isa. lx. 1.) And may those who step forth to rescue her from her present state of Popish thraldom, be encouraged in the work, remembering the Lord, whose "word is sure," hath proclaimed by the mouth of his prophet, "When the enemy shall come in like a flood, the Spirit of the Lord shall lift up a standard against him." (Isa. lix. 19.)

CHAPTER IV.

State of Christianity in Britain after the Death of Lucius, till the Dioclesian Persecution.—Martyrdom of Alban.—Constantine the Great ascends the Imperial Throne.—General Character of the Church universal at that time.—Council of Arles.

DURING the period of eighty years which followed the death of Lucius, scanty is the information which can be gathered respecting the British Church. Nevertheless, enough can be collected from our own and foreign authors, to satisfy us, that the Christian religion not only outwardly flourished, but that its professors remained firm in the faith, without apostasy or corruption, enjoying a happy exemption from the several doctrinal errors that afflicted other parts of the Church. Meanwhile, in Asia and Egypt, several heretics had appeared, who propounded various dogmas, which greatly obstructed the progress of the Gospel; but the Christians of Britain were saved from them by their great distance from the scene, and by their insular situation. They continued long to enjoy the light of the Gospel in all its primitive purity, and this contributed, not a little, both to the internal prosperity and to the external safety of the infant Church of Britain, and preserved it from many calamities which befel other Churches, which were infested with these heresies. The Christian religion, which had been silently and gradually extending itself in Britain during the second and third centuries, was to have the doubt and uncertainty in which its progress had been veiled, cleared away by the fires of affliction, proceeding from a fierce and cruel persecution. The authentic records of this calamity afford us important information respecting the conduct of the Christians, and the privileges which they had enjoyed.

[A. D. 303.] This storm broke out in the reign of Diocletian, at Nicomedia, when an imperial edict was published, ordering " that the churches should be pulled down, and the holy Scriptures burnt; that the profession of Christianity should render men incapable of any office or post of honour; that they should be outlawed, and debarred from the privilege of maintaining an action; and that no pretence of nobility of birth should excuse them from being put to the torture." This persecution was not only calculated to call into exercise all the powers of the Government to break down and extirpate Christianity, but it was as extensive in its range as it was violent in its character. Reaching to every part of the Roman empire, its fury fell even on the remotely situated Christians of Britain. The account furnished by Gildas, the oldest British Church historian, is both instructive and affecting:—
" The churches (of Britain) were overthrown, all the copies of the holy Scriptures which could be found were to be burned in the streets, and the chosen pastors of God's Church butchered, together with their innocent sheep, in order that not a vestige, if possible, might remain in some provinces, of Christ's religion. What disgraceful flights then took place,—what slaughter and deaths were inflicted by way of punishment in divers shapes,—what dreadful apostasies from religion then occurred; and, on the contrary, what glorious crowns of martyrdom then were won,—what

raving fury was displayed by the persecutors, and patience on the part of the suffering saints, ecclesiastical history informs us: for the whole Church were crowding in a body to leave behind them the dark things of this world, and to make the best of their way to the happy mansions of heaven, as if to their proper homes."

This extract teaches us, that at this early period the Christian religion was widely disseminated among the population of Britain; that numerous churches had been erected, and, what is still more remarkable, that copies of the holy Scriptures had been generally circulated. This latter fact is worthy of great attention. It shows that the infant Church in this island was reared up in accordance with the gracious designs of God, built upon the foundation of the apostles and prophets, Jesus Christ himself being the chief corner stone. (Eph. ii. 20.) For it is not till a Church neglects, mutilates, or prohibits the volume of revealed truth, that it ceases to recognise the Lord Jesus Christ as the one Mediator between God and man.

Even this terrible scourge fell more lightly on Britain, than on the other provinces of the Roman empire. Constantius Chlorus, the father of Constantine the Great, was then the Governor of Britain; and, being friendly to the Christian cause, he appears to have done all that lay in his power to mitigate, although he had not the authority to resist altogether, the Imperial edict. Notwithstanding this favour, and although we hear of no executions at Eboracum, (York,) where Constantius resided, in other parts of the country the Royal mandate was acted upon. The first martyrdom of which we have any record, is that of Alban, who was executed at Verulamium, whereby the town afterwards obtained the name of this martyr, being called St. Alban's. Alban, it is stated, was a native of Verulamium, but had journeyed to Rome, and eventually had joined the Imperial army, and, until this persecution arose, is said to have been a heathen. But a Christian teacher,* who had fled to his house for shelter from the same, became the instrument of his conversion. Struck with the behaviour of his guest, who passed a great part of the night, as well as of the day, in watching and prayer, Alban began to inquire concerning his religion, until at length he was persuaded to become a decided Christian. He had enjoyed the company and instruction of this person only a few days, when the Roman General, hearing that a Christian teacher was concealed in Alban's house, sent a party of soldiers to take him. When these came, Alban presented himself to them instead of his guest and teacher, attired in the habit, or long coat, the latter usually wore, and was led before the judge. The magistrate, standing by the altar of the heathen gods, soon discovered that, instead of the person sought for; he had before him a well-known young and noble Roman soldier, and, enraged at his behaviour, commanded him instantly to sacrifice to the gods, and thus clear himself of the suspicion of his having harboured a Christian and abetted his escape. This Alban not only refused to do, but boldly avowed himself a convert to the persecuted faith, pronouncing the gods of Rome to be devils. He was adjudged to death, and, after

* Amphibulas. Supposed to be a monk of Caerleon, and who soon after suffered martyrdom, with several others, at Redburn, a town near Verulamium. Monks of those days were a class of religious persons very different to those who bore the appellation at a future period.

having been beaten with rods, was led forth to execution, escorted by the eagle-bannered legions of still Pagan Rome.

We cannot entirely rely on the accounts which have been given of the circumstances connected with this martyrdom. It is said, that the bridge over which it was necessary to pass to the scene of death, being quite filled with the multitude congregated to witness the execution; Alban, anxious to hasten the consummation, walked down to the stream, and lifting his eyes to heaven, the waters divided, and he passed over on the bed of the river. It is also stated, that the person appointed to act as executioner was so affected by this miracle and the Christian firmness and patience displayed by the martyr, that he refused to strike the blow, choosing rather to die as a Christian with Alban. Other prodigies are related to have taken place in connexion with this event; but, however these may partake of the superstitious invention of later and *much darker days*, no fact in the history of those times is better attested than the martyrdom of Alban.

Romanists sometimes tauntingly ask Protestants, Where was your religion before Luther's time?

Britons may unhesitatingly and exultingly reply, On the heights of Verulamium, when the blood of martyred Alban was shed thereon.

Aaron and Julius, two citizens of Caerleon, are also said to have suffered about this time at Redbourne.

Besides these aforenamed martyrs, many others of both sexes suffered in other places, who, when they had endured sundry torments, and their limbs had been torn in an unheard-of manner, yielded up their souls to God, to enjoy in the heavenly city a reward for the sufferings through which they had passed. Numbers of the *terrified clergy* fled to *Ireland*, and there found a secure asylum from the Diocletian persecution. The Lord Jehovah saw fit, after hell had thus been aroused to destroy the Primitive Church of Britain, and the blood of her martyred followers had flowed, to rebuke the destroyer of his servants,—to speak the word, and the tempest of persecution passed away. But the malice of Satan towards it remained, and we shall find he, for a season, changed his weapons; what that had not been able to effect, subtilty and fraud were hereafter to be employed to accomplish with more success.

When the persecution had raged in Britain two years, the Emperors Diocletian and Maximian resigned the imperial dignity, and were succeeded by Constantius Chlorus and Galerius, who had been some time before created Cæsars. The new sovereigns divided the Roman empire between them, Galerius taking the east, and Constantius the west. Immediately on assuming the imperial purple, Constantius ordered the persecution of Christians to cease in his dominions, soon after which he was taken ill, and died at York.

[A.D. 313.] His son Constantine, surnamed the Great, (who had reached York in time to see the Emperor expire,) succeeded his father, and ascended the Imperial throne at that place.

The persecution of Diocletian, during its continuance here, must have retarded, in some measure, the progress of the truth; but the favourable countenance of Constantine made ample compensation for this, and opened up bright and cheering prospects to the British Church. From this time the Christian faith began to repair those injuries. "Christ's young disciples," says Gildas, "after so long and wintry a night, began to behold the genial light of heaven. They rebuilt the churches, which had been levelled to the ground: Christ's sons rejoice, as it were, in the fostering bosom of a mother."

At this date the great battle took place between Constantine and Maxentius, at a short distance from Rome, which, by the total defeat of the latter, gave the conqueror and his colleague Licinius the undisputed empire of the world. Immediately after this victory, Constantine cordially avowed himself a Christian, and the two sovereigns granted to the Christians a full power of living according to their own laws and institutions; which power was specified still more clearly, in another edict, drawn up at Milan in the following year. Public Ecclesiastical associations had been at first confined to the Greeks, but they soon became universal, and were formed wherever the Gospel was planted. To these assemblies, in which the deputies, or Commissioners of several Churches, consulted together, the name of "Synods" was appropriated by the Greeks, and that of "councils" by the Latins; and the laws or regulations enacted at them were called "canons," or "rules."

These councils, of which we cannot find the slightest trace before the middle of the second century, changed the whole face of the Church, and gave it an unknown form; for by them the ancient privileges of the people were considerably diminished, and the power and authority of the bishops greatly augmented. The humility and prudence of these early pious prelates prevented their assuming the power which their successors afterwards obtained. Bishops at their first appearance in these general councils acknowledged that they were no more than the delegates of their respective Churches, and that they acted in the name and by the appointment of the people. But in later councils this humble tone was changed, the limits of their authority were imperceptibly extended, their influence was turned into dominion, and their counsel into law, and, at length, they openly asserted that Christ had empowered them to prescribe to his people authoritative rules of faith and manners. Then followed the gradual abolition of that perfect equality which prevailed amongst all bishops in the primitive times, and human pride and ambition at last formed a new dignity, (A.D. 385,) investing the Bishop of Rome with the title and authority of " Prince of Patriarchs." It is evident that the wide extent of the Roman empire tended to foster and promote much of this arrangement in the Church, and almost the whole interruption of the primitive government of the Church may be traced to an intentional or accidental copying of the political divisions and magistracies of the empire, which, as the spirit and genius of the Gospel were lost sight of; ended in the erection of an universal and absolute spiritual monarchy in the person of the Pope, which, whatever may be said of intermediate points, stands out as an awful and profane contrast to all that is scriptural and divine in the economy of the primitive Church. The alterations alluded to in the constitution and government of the Churches were, however, more gradually introduced into Britain than into the more central parts of the Roman empire.

One of the first councils called together under the auspices of Constantine met at Arles, in the south of France; it consisted of bishops, presbyters, and deacons. The signatures of the British prelates of York, London, and Caerleon (as the head of the third Roman province in the island) being subscribed to the Acts of this

Council, must be admitted as a proof of the wide extent of Christian influence in the island at this period, and also of the prosperous and established character of her Church. But the most important branch of the information furnished by the records of this Council, respects the manner, in which it treated the Bishop of Rome. The Christian fathers assembled at Arles, (amongst whom the three aforesaid British prelates were numbered,) in sending him a copy of the Canons they had enacted; write, that they would have been glad of the company of their brother of Rome. They did *not* ask his confirmation of what they had done, they only transmitted their Canons to him, with the plain declaration "that they had already been settled by common consent, and were sent to him to make them more public." This historical fact is destructive to the future power the Pope assumed as the successor of St. Peter, and which he claimed as an inherent dignity attached to that see.*

* Appendix, No. 2.

CHAPTER V.

State of the Church during the Reign of Constantine the Great.—Remarks thereon.—Pelagian Heresy.—Ireland.

[A.D. 306.] WHEN we look at the external appearance of Christianity at this period, either in Britain or on the Continent, nothing can be more splendid or cheering. Constantine the Great, favourable to Britain from early associations and education, ascends the Imperial throne at York, and exhibits himself on the page of history, as full of real zeal that the only Divine religion should prosper under his government. By edicts he restores everything to the Church; he summons them to assemble in general council; he indemnifies those who had suffered; honours pastors; erects churches, and is aided therein by his mother, Helena, who fills the whole Roman empire with the tale of her munificent acts in support of Christianity. It may seem invidious to cast a shade on this picture, yet all this, if sound Christian principle is wanting, is but form and shadow. External piety certainly flourished, but genuine spiritual Christianity gradually withered, as the primitive form of Church government was departed from by the edicts of Constantine, summoning general councils of the Church.

The British Bishops, at this period, appear to have been in indigent circumstances, and did not benefit much from the famous edict Constantine published at Rome, which gave liberty to persons of all ranks to leave by will as great a portion of their estates as they pleased, to the Church. At Rome, and other wealthy cities, this decree greatly enriched the clergy by the liberal donations of opulent persons. But as Christians of this island were not so wealthy as those of some other countries, riches did not flow into the British Churches with so rapid a tide as elsewhere.

The pious mind which rejoices that the flames of persecution were extinguished, will now have to mourn over the introduction of erroneous doctrine* and religious controversy; which sprung from the twin evils of Arianism, and Pelagianism, spreading their poison through the Churches. The first heresy which seems to blot the page of Britain's Church history is allowed to be the Arian, which originated from Arius, a presbyter of Alexandria, and was intended to rob Christ of his glory and divinity. Bede tells us, that "peace continued in Britain until the time of the Arian madness, which, having corrupted the whole world, infested this island also, so far removed from the rest of the world, with the poison of its errors." Constantine summoned a general council of the Bishops, [A.D. 325,] from every quarter of the empire, to assemble at Nice, in Bithynia, on the Arian controversy. The British prelates attended the summons. The decision of this council was most important, and calculated to exercise a great and salutary influence on the Church through all ages. A Creed was drawn up by their authority, and published under their sanction, which exhibits, as fully as language can, a clear, distinct, and correct view of the divinity of the Son of God, and thereby condemned the erroneous ideas promulgated by Arius. The heresy not being extirpated,

* See page 34.

another general council [A.D. 347] was summoned by Constantine, at Sardica, in Bithynia, when, it seems, the British prelates were again present, three being in such circumstances that they permitted the charges of their journey to be defrayed by the Emperor, and they all concurred with the other bishops in the further condemnation of Arius and the principles he maintained.

The purity of the British Churches at this time is attested by St. Hilary, who, in an address forwarded to them and other bishops, thus writes:—" I congratulate you upon having remained undefiled in the Lord, and untainted by all the contagion of detestable heresy. Oh, the unshaken stedfastness of your glorious conscience! Oh, house, firm on the foundation of the faithful rock! Oh, the unimpaired and unmoved constancy of your uncontaminated will!" While these events were passing in the Church which ultimately so materially changed its aspect from one of primitive simplicity to that of disturbed controversy, the political affairs of the island also underwent a complete revolution. The Roman empire was tottering; the Britons seized on the opportunity thus offered them to throw off the yoke; the Romans took their final departure [A.D. 408] from hence; and not long after their empire was no more.

The Church was now universally placed in circumstances of great danger. Erroneous doctrines had been introduced, and troubled her pristine harmony; the clergy did not all stand firm, but fell under various temptations,—none perhaps, more to be deplored than the extent to which the simplicity of the early ages of Christianity, yielded to the expediency of burdening it with pompous ceremonies, under the pretext of gaining over the Heathen to embrace the cross of Christ. The poverty of the British Christians was, perhaps, the means of preserving them from the excesses other Churches plunged into.

[A.D. 401.] It was, however, about the beginning of the fifth century, that a new heresy was universally introduced throughout the Churches, by a Briton. He was a native of Wales, and his real name was Morgan (signifying sea-born, or near the sea); in his own time he was also known by the name of Brito; the Latins called him Pelagius, from a Greek word of the same signification. He studied at the celebrated monastery of Bangor, (a word implying college,) near Chester, where he resided as a lay monk, but, following the fashion of those times, resolved on removing to Rome. It was *not* till after his residence there that his orthodoxy appears to have been doubted; nor did his heterodoxy, it is supposed, publicly exhibit itself till late in life, and in the diffusion of this, he manifested that peculiar dexterity which has been common to all holders of erroneous doctrine, from the commencement of their appearance even to our own days. Whilst he laid open to his *converts the whole mystery of his doctrine*, he only imparted to others so much as might be more calculated to *ensnare*, introducing his views under the modest appearance of *queries*. At Rome, he found a powerful coadjutor in Celestius, an Hibernian Scot. They travelled far and wide on the Continent, but do not appear to have ever revisited Britain, a foreign bishop, named Agricola, importing the error hither. Arius had opposed the Divinity of Christ: the principles of Pelagius tended to give to fallen man an absurd, unnatural, and deceitful elevation. Both were false; both were awful perversions of Divine mercy, and dreadful denials of Divine truth. It has been thought, and with some show of reason, that the

Pelagian errors were received with greater avidity than the Arian, in Gaul and Britain, on account of their accordance with some of the doctrines of the Druids. The British clergy generally do not appear to have been at first led away by them, but being unable to oppose their growing influence in the island, they solicited assistance from Gaul; from whence Germanus, Bishop of Auxerre, and Lupus, Bishop of Troyes, were despatched to Britain. The promoters of the heresy at first kept out of the way, but at last they determined to risk a public dispute. "The fame of this conference drew abundance of people together, who came both to hear and to see; and the spot chosen for the occasion was Verulam (St. Alban's), then one of the chief cities of Britain. The contending parties were very different in their temper, figure, and furniture; one side relied on Divine aid, the other presumed on their own abilities; piety appeared in one, pride in the other party; Christ was for the first, Pelagius for the other."

[A.D. 429.] The result, however, was most satisfactory, for before an assembled multitude the pride of the Pelagians was mortified, and their sophistry exposed; and the people gave sentence by their acclamations, and could scarcely be restrained from beating them. Germanus and Lupus visited various parts of the island, preaching, not only in the churches, but sometimes in the fields and highways; and thus the orthodox were confirmed, and some of those who had been misled were reclaimed.

While Germanus and Lupus were thus engaged, we find the Saxons* and Picts had made an incursion into

---

* Some straggling volunteers of that nation, who came over to pillage, of their own accord, a few years before they were solemnly invited hither by the Jutish chieftains Hengist and Horsa, whom Vortigern had called in to support his authority.

Britain, whose inhabitants called to their aid these pious bishops, which led to their granting it to them, and facing the common foe at Mold, in Flintshire; and from the occurrence of the name Mærgarmon (the field of Germanus), in that parish, Archbishop Usher imagined it to have been the scene of the celebrated "Alleluiatic victory." It was in the season of Lent that this battle is supposed to have taken place, where, while engaged in baptizing the crowds who had flocked thither for the rite, and a church of boughs had been erected for the feast of the resurrection of our Lord, the whole was turned into a military camp. Germanus, with fortitude, directed the Britons how to act, and also faithfully to repeat his words. He advanced to meet the foe, bearing in his hands the standard. The enemy came on securely; the priests three times cried "Hallelujah!" A universal shout of the same word from the Britons followed, and the hills resounding the echo on all sides, the assailants were seized with a sudden panic, and fled. That a battle was fought at that spot, under circumstances which were afterwards improved into a miracle, is not improbable. After this event, Germanus and Lupus, having returned to Gaul, the British Churches for some time proceeded in regularity and good order. But Pelagianism, though defeated, was not destroyed; and Germanus was once more summoned hither; and he complied, being, on this occasion, accompanied by Severus, Bishop of Treves. Under their exertions the heresy again yielded. Germanus visited various parts of the island; and indisputable traces of his progress are to be found in Wales and Cornwall; yet, it is much to be feared, that amidst his very valuable services, the influence of the Gallic opinions and predilections he intro-

duced, ultimately tended to the injury of British Christianity. To Germanus is ascribed the introduction into the British Churches of the Gallican Liturgy.*
He also is the person who, it is supposed, first consecrated in Britain nuns to that degree of religious life, which on the Continent, seems to have been then required of females desirous of devoting their lives to God. To Germanus is also attributed the division of certain districts in Wales into parishes. His influence in that principality appears to have been very great, promoted perhaps by his lineage, and family connexion with some of its leading chieftains.

Celestius, the coadjutor whom Pelagius had found at Rome for the dissemination of his heresy, had, like himself, it appears, received a sound Christian education in Ireland, his native country. Three letters to his parents are extant, which not only imply that they were Christians, but likewise that such professors formed a large community in that country. These letters were written in the form, as we are told, of little books, and full of such piety as to make them necessary to all who loved God. Their date is A.D. 369, and unquestionably point to a full reception of Christianity into Ireland, even at a much earlier date, and were evidently written before his falling into the grievous errors of Pelagianism. The celebrated Sedulius, the ablest opponent, perhaps, to be found to the arrogant and presumptuous heresy of Pelagius, was also an Irishman, and, of course, contemporary with Celestius. As a missionary, he travelled through France, Italy, Asia, and Achaia. He wrote several works in prose and verse. "How profoundly skilled Sedulius was in the leading doctrines of the Gospel,

* See Appendix, No. 6.

may be inferred," says the able historian of Ireland, "from the clearness, conciseness, and appositeness of his remarks, critically comparing Scripture with itself, according to the analogy of faith. He was, indeed, an honour to his country, and a bright luminary in the orthodox Church of his age. Surely the country that produced such scholars as Celestius and Sedulius, at that early date (A. D. 370), must have arrived at a high state of mental civilization."

We learn from Dr. O'Hallaron (a distinguished Roman Catholic antiquary), that at the period of which we are now speaking, and when Christianity was making such rapid progress in Ireland, "a most uncompromising enmity existed in the minds of the Irish people against everything connected with Rome." It is unreasonable, therefore, to suppose, that from Rome they had received that Christian instruction which had broken down their heathen superstition, dissolved their former religion, and produced such an important revolution in the minds of all, as ultimately to lead them, with one consent, to profess themselves Christians. Archbishop Usher states, that the profession and practice of Christianity, in the *fifth century, in Ireland, varied very little from that of the present Established Church of England and Ireland.*

Though not connected with the subject, in closing this chapter, it is worthy of remark, that the Pelagian heresy on the Continent met with the decided opposition of St. Augustine and St. Jerome.

CHAPTER VI.

Christian Biography.—St. Patrick.—Ireland.—Spiritual Condition of the British Church at conclusion of the Fifth Century.

IN the foregoing chapter, a brief outline was given of the Pelagian heresy, and the state of Christianity in Ireland at that time. We will now take a retrospective notice of some of the leading Christian individuals who lived during, and about, that period, and whose biography may be likely to throw any light on the religious history of Britain. For this purpose we will first mention Keby. This truly Christian prince was the son of Solomon, King of Cornwall, and was born about A.D. 325. Keby, having resolved to devote himself entirely to the study and teaching of Christianity, was eventually ordained and consecrated a Bishop by the famous Hilary, of Poictiers, at whose death he returned to Cornwall, not to reign, but to devote the residue of his life to religion; and there is reason to suppose that he established himself for that purpose at Tregoney.

[A.D. 369.] Very distressing political and family circumstances induced Keby to flee from Cornwall. Having spent four years in Ireland, he ultimately retired to the Isle of Anglesea. "There," says Leland, "he fixed his abode, an humble one at first; but the King of the isle, in pity to the poorness of it, liberally presented him with a castle, which stood in the vicinity; and there he ended his days, giving his name to the

Church and village." From the sanctity of his life, the headland which is immediately opposite to Ireland, and near which he lived, was called Holy Head, a name which it yet retains. Keby (who, in after-times, was called St. Keby) is said to have exerted himself with great success against Pelagianism. His life appears to have been eminently useful and holy; yet how slender is the information which history has preserved respecting it! How different, in this particular, from the tempest-tongue of fame, announcing the blasting progress of the warrior, or gilding with false glory the unholy rage of ambition! Yet there is a day approaching, when it shall not be so.

It was about A.D. 420, that Ninius, or Ninian, who was a native of North Wales, (where the British Church was then flourishing,) devoted himself to the perilous work of carrying the faith of Christ among the Southern Picts, who were, at that time, in possession of the northern part of what is now called England. Ninian penetrated into Caledonia (Scotland), where he founded a Bishopric at Whitherne, in Galloway, and built a church, which is the earliest record we have of a stone church, which, according to Bede, "was not usual among the Britons;" and it long remained a monument of his successful labours. Gildas describes these people, to whom St. Ninian devoted his exertions, "as a very savage race, wearing more hair on their faces than they had clothes on their bodies;" yet, it is reported, that he was the means of converting many of these barbarians from their idolatry to the worship of the true God. About the same period lived also Fastidius, a British Bishop, who resided at London. His name is now chiefly remarkable as being the only Christian teacher, amongst the ancient Britons, of whom any doctrinal treatise remains. He also left a short piece on "The Character of a Christian Life," addressed to a pious widow, named Fatalis; in which, after modestly excusing his own want of knowledge and little skill, and begging her "to accept his household bread, since he cannot offer her the finest flour," he shows, with "very plain and good arguments, that Christians are called to imitate Him whom they worship; that, without a life of piety and uprightness, it is vain to presume on the mercy of God, or boast of the name of Christian; and that it was always the rule of God's dealing with mankind to love righteousness and hate iniquity." In ending his treatise, he thus expresses his advice to her:—"Be holy, humble, and quiet, and employed, without ceasing, in works of mercy and righteousness: above all, ever study the commandments of your Lord; earnestly give yourself to prayers and psalms, that if it be possible, no one may ever find you employed but in reading or in prayer. And when you are so employed, remember me."

[A.D. 431.] At this date, *the first* effort was made on the part of the Roman See, to establish a mission in Ireland, under the direction of Palladius, for the ostensible purpose of strengthening and assisting those of the nation who were already believers; but it proved a complete failure. The Irish clergy and people of that day would *not* listen to his foreign commission, and therefore they unceremoniously dismissed the Pope's delegate, *who retired from the island after a stay of only three weeks.*

We have now arrived at the period when the name of one must be brought forward to whom has been by some writers falsely attributed the first conversion of the Irish to Christianity; but the details which have already been placed before us will have established that circumstance to have been brought about by other persons, and in much earlier days. The celebrated individual, whose memory has been handed down to our times as St. Patrick, confirms, by his writings, the assertion of many other authors, that he was born (A. D. 372) in North Britain,—some state at Kirkpatrick, in Caledonia (Scotland),* and that his father was Calpurnius, a deacon, and his grandfather a priest, and that his uncle was St. Martin, Bishop of Tours. When he was sixteen years of age, he was taken prisoner by pirates, and brought to Ireland, where he continued six years, when, by some means, he effected his escape, and returned to his native country, having, during his captivity, been converted to the faith of Christ, and having made himself well acquainted with the language and manners of the people of Ireland. From this period he is said to have had an intense desire to be employed as a missionary in Ireland. To prepare himself for this work, he first passed into France, and studied under his uncle, Martin, of Tours.

* There exists a Welsh tradition respecting this great Apostle of Ireland, who, according to the Silurian Catalogue of Saints, was the son of Mawon, and a native of Gwyr, or Gower, in Glamorganshire; and, under the name of Padrig, was the first Principal of the College of Caermorgan. It is unnecessary to enter further into these particulars, for until the evidence of his connexion with the Principality is better established, they do not overthrow the testimony of other authors. The historical facts which have been, and will be, placed in this little Volume before the reader respecting the Irish Church, will be selected almost entirely from Murray's "History of Ireland and her Church," and in matters of peculiar importance that author's own words will be adhered to.

He received ordination as presbyter from Germanus, Bishop of Auxerre.

[A.D. 429.] Having accompanied Germanus and Lupus on their already-mentioned first mission into Britain, his former desire for the spiritual instruction of the Irish seems to have revived with increased ardour. Having preached in Britain with great success, in opposition to the Pelagian heresy, he received consecration as a bishop from the above-named prelates, and then passed over to Ireland, and became one of the most successful missionaries that ever appeared in the isle of Erin.*

It is computed with much probability, that after long and laborious wanderings in that country, and

---

* St. Patrick, it appears, preached in Wales with great effect; and as he was subsequently, while there, consecrated bishop by Germanus, whose family connexions were from that part, these incidental circumstances may have given rise to the tradition of his own Welsh extraction. He embarked for Ireland, it is supposed, from Wales. A chapel was dedicated to him in the parish of St. David's, Pembrokeshire, on the spot where, it is recorded, an angel appeared to him, and commanded him to preach the Gospel in Ireland. (Rees' "Welsh Saints.")

St. Patrick receiving consecration as a bishop from Germanus and Lupus while in Wales, is another proof, that the statements of Romish authors, in connexion with the Church history of Ireland, are not to be relied on, in matters connected with the Papacy, for they represent that he obtained it while at Rome, which place, the *best authorities state, he never visited.*

The hymn of Feich also opposes the Roman hypothesis. In the first four stanzas we have the parentage of the apostle, his captivity and flight from Ireland; then the story proceeds as follows:—

> "He traversed the whole of Albion;
> He crossed the sea, it was a happy voyage;
> And he took up his abode with German,
> Far away to the south of Armorica.

after he had established the Church on the best foundation which circumstances permitted, he bent his way towards the north, with the intention of establishing a primatical see, and confirming his labours by a body of canons. With this view, he reached the place then called Denein Sailrach, and since Armagh. From the chief of this district he obtained possession of an extensive tract of land, and founded a city upon it, large in compass and beautiful in situation, with monastery, cathedral, schools, &c., and resolved to establish it as the primatical see of the Irish Church. This foundation, it is stated, took place in 445. Here, and at his favourite retreat at Sabhul, he probably spent the remainder of his life. "The Canons" universally ascribed to him are supposed to have been ordained at a synod held in Armagh. Amongst the last of his acts was a short narrative of his life, under the title of "Confession." It is represented as a simple, characteristic, often-affecting and unpretending document. In speaking of approaching death, he returns thanks for the mercies of God to himself and the Irish, &c. He was seized with his last illness at

> "Among the isles of the Tuscan sea,
> There he abode, as I pronounce;
> He studied the Canons with German,
> Thus it is that the Churches testify.
>
> "To the land of Erin he returned,
> The angels of God inviting him;
> Often had he seen in visions
> That he should come once more to Erin."

Through the whole piece Italy is omitted, and in a narrative, so orderly and circumstantial as this is, omission is equivalent to exclusion.

Saul, or Sabhul, near Downpatrick, and wishing to die at Armagh, he attempted the journey, but was compelled, by his complaint, to return, and he breathed his last on the 17th of March, 493.*

Great as were the services St. Patrick rendered to the Irish nation, to him must be attributed the introduction of monachism in its mildest form into that country, and for which he probably derived a predilection from his uncle, St. Martin, Bishop of Tours, and from the influence also of Germanus. St. Patrick's gravity, simplicity, wisdom, moderation, piety, and just views still beautifully gleam through the legendary accounts handed down to our times, sadly disguised as they are, by the superstitious fancies of some of his biographers.

To the flourishing state of religion and letters in Ireland, after the apostolic labours of Sedulius and Patrick, honourable and impartial testimony is borne. The disciples of these men profited so notably, it is recorded, in Christianity, that, in succeeding ages, none were held more holy or more learned than the Irish clergy, insomuch that they sent out *swarms of devoted missionaries into every part of Europe*. According to the language of Dr. Johnson, *Ireland*, during the sixth, seventh, eighth, and part of the ninth centuries, was "*the school of the West.*"

---

* The traditionary records of the Isle of Man inform us that St. Patrick, landing there in his second voyage to Ireland, succeeded in founding its Episcopal see, and, through a great variety of changing circumstances in the government and possession of the island during the period of 1400 years, it has enjoyed an uninterrupted course of separate and independent jurisdiction. The bishop is appointed direct from the Crown, not requiring a *congé d'élire* to be issued to the Chapter.

In further tracing her Church history, we shall find her mitred missionaries were the honoured instruments in the hands of God, of evangelizing the greater part of Saxon England and Scotland: and, not content with this, she extended " the cords of her tent " over almost every part of the Continent of Europe. Let the young reader stand, in imagination, on the top of Mount St. Gothard (or pause, if ever he visits the spot), where her house of refuge still remains, and looking to the north, to the south, to the east, and to the west, he will be able to trace, with the map of Europe in his hands, the footsteps of the Irish missionaries through France, Germany, Switzerland, and Italy, imparting to the inhabitants of these extensive regions, the blessings of pure religion and moral civilization. Her seminaries and churches at home, during the same period, were the asylum of learned men from all parts of Europe. Kings' sons were among her honourable pupils. Her colleges and churches were scattered from Iona, in North Britain, to Bobbio, in Italy: all proclaim the same fact, that Ireland was the focus, from which the light of Divine truth was shed over the greater part of the continent of Europe.

The fifth century was the period when the Irish Christians directed their attention and exertions so especially to Cornwall, and poured into it such numerous missionaries, that it is still notorious for the number of churches dedicated to their memory. The ancient church of Perranzabuloe, or St. Piran, lately disinterred from its grave of sand on the coast of Cornwall, and which is conjectured to have been one of the earliest British churches that was built of stone, is yet an existing monument of the efforts, or effect of the exertions made by the Irish for the establishment of Christianity in those early days in that part of England. Piran, to whom this church seems to have been dedicated, or through whom it was built, arrived, with his mother and several other missionaries, from Ireland, their native country, about A.D. 450, and devoted their lives and labours to impart religious knowledge to the surrounding population. Doubtless those exertions were blessed, or no churches would have been required. The remains, it is supposed, of Piran and of his mother were, a few years ago, found under the altar,* when the church was cleared from the sand, wherewith the waves of the Atlantic had for centuries kept it concealed. Further testimony to the exertions of Irish missionaries in this land could be adduced, if it were deemed a matter of real moment to trace them further in these pages.

On examining into the spiritual state of the British Church and her converts, at the close of the fifth century, the fact cannot be concealed, that, however outwardly advantageous, the step taken by the British clergy of calling in Germanus and Lupus from Gaul, to suppress the Pelagian heresy might, at the time, have appeared,—it ultimately proved an unwise measure, and tended to the vital injury of British Christianity; and the same can be easily accounted for by the evidence we have, that at that time, the continental Churches had already departed from apostolic simplicity; and had adopted rites, ceremonies, and institutions which, though few and unimportant in themselves, rather encumbered, than promoted the progress of Gospel truth and genuine religion. Germanus, with Lupus and his other companions, certainly introduced

* This assertion is not to be entirely depended on; it rather opens a question for doubt to the antiquarian.

these innovations into Britain; for it is an undoubted fact, that he was the first to establish monasteries and to consecrate nuns; steps which paved the way for greater religious evils. Many persons, also, who then professed to have abandoned Heathenism, were unfaithful to their high calling as Christians, and remained strangers to the constraining influence of genuine spiritual Christianity. This religious declension had probably been nurtured by the great scarcity of the Holy Scriptures after the Diocletian persecution, when so many were destroyed; for if the Bible had been within the reach of the populace, it might have warned them against such departures in doctrine and practice, by the examples of the apostles. The degenerate condition of the Church, and the circumstances with which it was then surrounded, seemed to threaten it with the divine warning of God sent unto the Church of Ephesus: "Remember from whence thou art fallen, and repent, and do thy first works; or else I will come quickly, and will remove thy candlestick out of his place, except thou repent;" (Rev. ii. 5);—a warning applicable to all portions and all ages of the Christian Church, and more especially to our own at this time. Even in those days, some faithful and zealous ministers urged this sound advice with impassioned ardour, but still true religion declined, and ultimately the fearful consequences were felt. The Lord sent his judgments, and the fairest portion of Britain soon fell under the scourge of Pagan, and finally beneath that of Papal conquerors!

CHAPTER VII.

Departure of Roman Legions.—Picts and Scots.—Vortigern.—Arrival and Struggles with Angles and Saxons.—Biographical Sketches of distinguished Christians.—Dubricius, David, Culdees, Columba, Irish Missionaries.

WE must now resume the historical and connecting link of these inquiries, by observing that the turbulent and cloudy aspect of Britain's social and political condition, after the withdrawal of the Roman legions, (independent of the causes already alluded to in the preceding chapter), must have been such as would little favour the growth of Christianity. Delivered from the presence of Roman governors, powerful chiefs, warring with each other, eventually placed the most daring or successful at the head of various tribes: these efforts for ascendancy meanwhile keeping the population in a state of feverish excitement.

The Picts took advantage of these domestic broils amongst the Britons to pour into the country, on every suitable or convenient opportunity, to carry off plunder. The Britons, though certainly brave and valorous in petty and local quarrels, having been accustomed to Roman leaders in war, when deprived of their guidance, became, in national undertakings, disunited, and, of course, powerless. The reflections, therefore, of pusillanimity which some writers have cast on them are undeserved, and the assistance which was first sought from Rome (A. D. 446), and subsequently was obtained from others by Vortigern, a Silurian chief, when he had become Pendragon * of the southern and eastern parts of the island, ought *not* to have been commented on as a *national* act, but as that of some particular district. Such was the political character of Britain at the time when the already-described Pelagian heresy made its appearance, and Germanus and Lupus visited the country, to try and suppress it.

It is supposed that Vortigern—actuated by selfish and unworthy motives, and anticipating that Ambrosius Aurelius, a chieftain of Imperial descent, whom many desired to raise to the supreme command, would accede to that wish—connived at the settlement of Hengist and Horsa, two Jutish chiefs or pirates, in the Isle of Thanet, for the ostensible purpose of assisting him against the Picts. This impolitic step, it is well known, gave Saxon marauders a footing in the country, which finally led to the subjugation of the fairest portion of it to their yoke. These piratical conquerors of Britain were Pagans, composed of a motley multitude drawn from three distinct continental tribes, distinguished amongst historians as Jutes, Angles, and Saxons, but more familiar to ourselves under the general appellation of Saxons, or Anglo-Saxons. Gradually did these intruders and assailants press forward, as the inhabitants either fled before them or perished by the sword, which cut off *their remembrance* from the earth, and likewise the *recollection* of their *sufferings* and *resistance*. How could the Britons deal with the heathenish doctrines and worship of their conquerors? Were they in a position to exhort or to reclaim? Let us for a moment consider with what feelings a British Christian would witness a Saxon

* *i. e.*, the leading king.

chief measuring out and appropriating the fields and possessions which had belonged to himself and his sires; while he and his children were doomed, as slaves, to cultivate, for the use of his usurping lord, that very land. Yet how much greater would be the pain—how much keener the mental anguish, when he beheld the brutal orgies of their fresh-imported gods, Woden and Thor, celebrated; where he, under the ministry and guidance of some Christian teacher, had worshipped the true and living God—the God of his forefathers! This enslaved possessor of the holy faith, could henceforth, only hope to worship Jehovah by stealth and in solitude, or by the contemptuous sufferance of proud and ignorant idolaters. This, however, was the real condition of a people now accused by some writers and persons * of not attempting the conversion of their conquerors.

Although we have already mentioned, that before these times of purifying and refining sufferings came, there had been a general departure in the Church, from the principles and practice of genuine religion and godliness, yet we cannot but hope, that many, very many of those backsliding wanderers were brought back unto repentance, by the pressure of those afflictions before they perished by the Saxon sword; or, abandoning their homes, fled into the mountain fastnesses of Scotland and Wales, or the remote parts of the western peninsula of the island.

The struggle between the invaders and the Britons was not either of short duration; it extended over

* What excuse can these reproachers of the conquered race of pristine Britons offer for the millions of their own long-subjugated fellow-subjects in British India being still permitted to remain heathens?

a period of near a century and a half; and the traces yet existing of various scenes of battle between them testify, that to the continually reinforced battalions of the Saxons, and their confederates from the wide space of Europe, the Britons must have offered great resistance, and have defended their patrimonial inheritance not only with skill but courage. While the Saxons were thus consolidating their power, forming distinct kingdoms, and spreading the influence of their heathenish belief with the progress of their arms, the Lord God of Hosts was pleased to give a mighty impulse to pure religion, amongst the scattered remnants of the British Church. The researches of the historian and antiquary furnish us with proofs, that under the benign influence of genuine Christianity, many persons of rank, intelligence, and property, consecrated themselves, in the remote and unapproachable localities of Scotland, Wales, and Cornwall, to the service of God, and became the instruments of maintaining and promoting therein the knowledge of salvation.

As war is not our theme, but the progress of the Gospel of peace, we will say no more on political events, but turn our attention to the most prominent individuals who, during these eventful times, thus upheld the cross of Christ. Accordingly, the first who seems to claim our attention is the celebrated Dubricius, Archbishop of Caerleon. This distinguished person is represented as being a grandson of Brychan, who was originally an Irish missionary, amongst a colony of his own countrymen, who had settled in North Wales; but who eventually became the patriarch of a distinguished race of Welsh kings, princes, and saints. Dubricius's early efforts seem to have been directed only to the dissemination of religious and other learning, as the first notice we have of him is in connexion with his famed seminary of Hentland on the Wye, where he had one thousand students, having another also at Moch Ross. He was consecrated Bishop of Llandaff by Germanus; and Ambrosius Aurelius, the powerful successor of Vortigern, materially assisted him in promoting the cause of Christianity, while, as a warrior, he sustained his own character for the space of fifty years.

Dubricius was ultimately created Archbishop of Caerleon, and there had the honour of crowning the far-famed King Arthur, of legendary and romantic history. At a great council, Dubricius appointed Sampson, an eminent divine, primate of the northern portion of Britain, who, establishing himself at York, was compelled by the Saxons to retire, and he fled to Armorica, in Gaul. He was succeeded by another Sampson, called the younger, whom Dubricius consecrated bishop at large; but he likewise was obliged to abandon his charge, and also took refuge in Armorica, where he eventually became Archbishop of Dole. This primate has been mentioned by writers as that "child of prayer," and at a council at Paris (A.D. 557) subscribed his name as "I, Sampson, a sinner and a bishop."

After a life of the greatest usefulness, Dubricius, at a very advanced age, convened a council, not only of the clergy but of the laity, at Brefi, in Cardiganshire, for the purpose of checking the insidious advances of Pelagian error. At this council Dubricius resigned the primacy of Caerleon, and withdrew to a monastery in the isle of Enlli, or Bardsey, where he died, A.D. 522. He was buried in the island, where his remains lay *uncanonized, unenshrined, and undisturbed, for six hundred years;* proving that, however great may have been the esteem in which the primitive British Christians held the memory of their holy men, they could not have worshipped their relics. Accordingly, when Urban, Bishop of Llandaff, had obtained the permission of princes and bishops to remove the remains of Dubricius to that cathedral, (A. D. 1120,) the history of the search proves, that his bones had been so little regarded, that, if obtained at all, they were found under those of numerous other bodies.

Dubricius, at the Council of Brefi, had resigned, with the full consent of the council of clergy and laity then assembled, the sacerdotal offices to David, who became the patron saint of Wales. He is also described as connected with distinguished persons; and to have been born near Menevia, or Menapia, now St. David's, in Pembrokeshire, and to have been baptized at Port Clais in that neighbourhood, by Albeus, Bishop of Munster, "who by Divine Providence had arrived at that time from Ireland." David is reported to have received his religious education in the school of Iltutus, and afterwards to have proceeded to that of Paulinus at Tygwyn ar Daf (now Whitlands, Carmarthenshire), where he is said to have spent ten years in the study of the Scriptures, having, previous to entering that seminary, been ordained presbyter.

In company with Padran and Teilo, his fellow-students, David visited Jerusalem, and they were there consecrated to the order of bishops, by the patriarch. After he had been appointed Archbishop of Wales, he obtained the consent of King Arthur to remove the seat of his sacred office from Caerleon to Menapia, thenceforth called St. David's. There he convened another council, where the principles of Pelagianism were again condemned, and provisions made for the benefit of the Church. This excellent man seems to have been equally talented and pious. His life appears to have been one of continued exertion in the defence and promotion of pure religion. He was revered in his own day, as an able and eminent minister of Christ. An ancient author, speaking of him, says, that "his holy life and bright example shine forth conspicuous to all. He instructed the people, both by his word and example. His preaching was most powerful, and his actions more so. The ornament of the religious, the life of the needy, the defence of the orphan, the support of widows, and the father of his pupils, making himself all things to all men, that he might win them to God."

We will thus close the testimony that accredited historians give of his character, and not touch on the fabulous legends invented respecting him by the monks of later ages, as they are only a mass of absurdity and profaneness. It is generally agreed that Wales was first divided into dioceses, during the time that David was Primate of that Principality, and that he died at Menapia, about A. D. 544 or 546.

[A.D. 500.] Before proceeding further in our biographical sketches, it appears desirable to inform the reader that about A.D. 500, a colony of the Scoti, or Irish, emigrating to Caledonia, took their name into the country now known as Scotland; and under which appellation, it may henceforth be more generally mentioned in the following pages. Some account must also be given respecting a religious order, which had existed in Ireland *one hundred years before* Patrick's mission for promoting Christianity in that country had been contemplated. This order, styled the Culdees, was perfectly independent of the See of Rome: their rule had been invented by a celebrated Bishop of Egypt, adopting the office of the Greek, and not the Roman; and even in their mode of tonsure * they differed from similar institutions in the Roman Church. This celebrated monastic order, though of Irish origin and nurture, was not destined to remain there in solitude. A leader was to appear, and transfer them to another, though a sister soil. Columba, the founder, or, rather, reviver of this order, was descended from the Royal family of Ireland, and likewise nearly allied to the King of Scotland,† and was born about A.D. 521. Exhibiting great quickness of parts, he was early committed to the care of a pious presbyter, and afterwards to that of two bishops, all of whom were charmed and surprised with the holiness and proficiency of their pupil. In the twenty-eighth year of his age, he founded the monastery of Durrogh, wherein he deposited a copy of the Evangelists which he had transcribed. Brilliant parts, and an untiring zeal in the service of religion, with a strain of powerful eloquence, exalted Columba's reputation amongst his countrymen to a degree scarcely inferior to that of an apostle. Such talents were too large to be confined within the narrow pale of a monkish cell: they were called forth to the regulation of State affairs, and in them he held as decided a superiority as in the cloister. Amidst this splendour of authority and of parts, it

* The form of shaving the heads of monks, to represent our Redeemer's crown of thorns.

† In those times noblemen were not seldom preachers of the Gospel.

would have been miraculous, if human weakness had not sometimes betrayed him into error; and it is supposed, that having instigated a war without a just cause, he abjured his native land by a voluntary exile, and imposed on himself a mission to the unconverted Picts. Of this event Bede thus speaks:—" In the year of our Lord 565, there came out of Ireland into Britain a presbyter and abbot, a monk in life and habits, very famous, by name Columba, to preach the Word of God to the provinces of the northern Picts." With twelve companions, or friends, Columba' landed at the isle of Hy, or Hi, near the confines of the Scottish and Pictish territories. " The northern Picts were separated," says Bede, " from the southern parts by steep and rugged mountains; for the southern Picts, who dwell on this side the mountain, had long before, as is reported, forsaken the errors of idolatry and embraced the truth by the preaching of Ninias, a holy man of the British nation." Columba was then in the forty-second year of his age, and he needed all that vigour of mind and body which he possessed, to meet the difficulties which stood opposed to the success of his mission. Idolatry, with no knowledge of its professors' language, stood foremost to confront his efforts. Notwithstanding all these obstacles of various descriptions placed before him, in the course of a few years the greater part of the Pictish kingdom was brought to a knowledge of the truth of Christianity, and many were savingly converted to God.

Monasteries, according to the rule of the Culdees, were built in many places, and churches generally established. Columba, as primate, superintended and directed all the affairs of the Pictish Churches, and many of the Scotch and Irish. He was revered from the monarch to the poorest of his subjects; when he walked abroad he was received with the highest demonstration of respect, crowds attending him wherever he went.* His monastery at Iona was, perhaps, the chief seminary of learning in Europe at that time, and supplied the world with divines and pastors. As a missionary himself his success seems almost unrivalled; his gifts and attainments were undoubtedly of a most superior order, but never could of themselves have produced such extraordinary results. For a satisfactory and practical solution of the matter we must regard the character of Columba as a Christian minister. Not resting in any measure of sanctity acquired in early life, he incessantly laboured after higher and higher degrees of it, to his latest days. Columba was so remarkable for the spirit and practice of prayer, that it forms a striking and important feature in his character; it seems to have been his invariable rule to undertake no work, to officiate in no ministerial duty, or to administer medicine, till he had first invoked the blessing of God. His devotional spirit, his prayerful communion with God, and consistent walk, formed upon the apostolic model, clearly account for the abundant success of all his religious under-

* His biographers refer the change of his name to Columcille to the religious feeling which seemed to ascribe every slight occurrence to special design. His exceeding meekness attracted the attention of the children of the neighbourhood, who were accustomed to see him coming forth to meet them at the gate of the monastery, in which he received his education; and by a fanciful adaptation, common enough to lively children, they called him "the Pigeon, or Dove, of the Church," which in Irish is Columna-cille. Others think, Columcille was given to him, in reference to his having founded so many monasteries, and to distinguish him from others of the same name.

takings,—in consequence of which the king of that part of the Pictish nation gave him the Isle of Hy, or Iona, one of the Hebrides, where he first landed; and it was there he built and founded his far-famed monastery, the abode and retreat from henceforth of the Culdees. Columba is spoken of as having promoted the monastic system, an excrescence engrafted on Christianity, but which had not at that time put on the unhealthy form it afterwards did. On the contrary, we find him sharply reproving a person who, by way of doing penance, affected to impose upon himself hardships, which neither God nor his spiritual guides required.

The zeal of the monks of Iona in disseminating knowledge and true religion in those days is indeed astonishing; it flamed amongst them in the bosom of age as well as in the veins of youth: we meet with their traces in every country of Europe, so much so, that it is observed, " all saints whose origin could not be traced were supposed to come from Ireland or Scotland;" and Bede confirms it all by stating, " the cure of souls was their great concern." It is also important to notice, that Columba and his followers, (the Culdees), were entirely guided by the Scriptures, and being led by the true light, they were saved from the many errors into which other societies and persons sank, who substituted the traditions, wisdom and inventions of men, for the truth and power of God. This eminent missionary, worn out with toil in the service of his Divine Master, died [A. D. 597] at Iona, aged seventy-five years, and lies interred in the island Abbey. Columba may be, perhaps, selected from amongst the departed faithful servants of the Lord, as the brightest and best example that can be placed before the present generation, either as a minister or missionary: for where can we find a fairer copy of the mind, spirit, and labouring zeal of the apostles of Christ? Can his piety be questioned, or his Christian pity to the fallen race of man be suspected? He was styled " Abbot Presbyter," and exercised an authority over the bishops of that part, though he never attained to the dignity himself: a clear proof that he did not consider a presbyter inferior to a bishop.

We have, in the foregoing pages, alluded to the number of Irish missionaries, afterwards styled saints, who devoted their lives, their all—for many of them were of noble birth—to the cause of God in Cornwall; but before we close the short account, which it seems necessary to give, for further fastening conviction of that fact on the mind and recollection of the reader, we must mention the names of a few more of them. Petrock was the son of a Welsh king; he travelled into Ireland for religious instruction, and then settled in Cornwall. A vessel from Ireland containing Christian teachers entered the harbour of Hayle; two were unfortunately slain, but the rest were protected and patronized, and their names were long, and some are still, associated with various localities. An Irish king, named Germork, having retired from the cares of royalty, was amongst them. St. Germorchus was a church named after him, and standing three miles from St. Michael's Mount. Hya, the daughter of an Irish nobleman; Budock, a hermit; Fingar, Burien, Carantoc, Piala, Crewenn, and others, in the same manner settled, and died, at the places which still bear their several names, and at which their piety and memory were for ages after greatly revered. Teilo, who had been consecrated at Jerusalem at the same time as St. David, and succeeded him in the primacy of Menapia, with consent of King Arthur, removed its see to Llandaff, leaving a suffragan at the former place. In the year 588 this eminent Bishop sailed, with a considerable company of Christian ministers and others, into Bretagne, on account of an epidemic which nearly desolated Wales, and touched at Cornwall, where he was well received by the king Gerrennius and his people. As they returned, seven years after, to the same port, they found King Gerrennius in the last agony of life, who, "when he had received the holy Sacrament from the hand of Teilo, departed in joy to the Lord."

Gildas "the wise," known amongst the Welsh writers under the name of Dneurin, demands notice, for he was the earliest of British historians, and appears to have been a person of real piety, though troubled with rather a morose and grumbling disposition. He is supposed to have been descended from a Bardic family, and to have been born about the year A.D. 520, and to have received his early education at the College of Lantwit major, Glamorganshire. In his valuable writings he feelingly deplores the miserable state of his country, and declaims severely against the vices and habits of both clergy and laity. The numerous quotations and expositions he has given from both the Old and New Testaments, must lead his readers to infer, that the contents of the sacred volume were deeply studied in the early British Colleges. Some of his writings are now to be met with in English, and are deeply interesting.

In no better way can we, perhaps, close these

biographical sketches of the principal or leading ministers who, during these years of Saxon struggle, laboured in the Lord's fold, and tried to keep together his persecuted and scattered flock, than by remarking, that even in that part of Britain which had been the actual seat of war for 150 years, we have satisfactory proof that Theanus, Bishop of London, did not leave his see till A.D. 586, only ten years before Augustine's arrival. He at that date fled with his clergy (and in company with Tadiaus, Archbishop of York) into Wales.

Feebly and imperfectly as the visible track of the British Church has been delineated in the foregoing pages, enough, it is to be hoped, has been exhibited to satisfy an unprejudiced reader, that from the apostolic age she has not ceased to exist. For, observe, the pristine king, Lucius, is allowed to have been the first sovereign in Europe, if not in the world, who paid homage to the name of Jesus; an earnest, it now almost appears to have been, of the Lord's continuing loving-kindness towards our nation and her people. Moreover, the first Roman Emperor who embraced Christianity, if not of British extraction,* was educated in this country, and so much associated with it, that he received the summons to ascend the Imperial throne at York. Further, the external evidence of the continued existence of a British Church, from those early days, is now apparent in every part of the western coast of our island; and from the north of Scotland to the

* According to the Welsh accounts, Helen, or Helena, the wife of his father, Constantius Chlorus, was the daughter of Coel, a British king. Perhaps she was Constantius Chlorus's second wife, and therefore Constantine's step-mother.

Land's End. It is proclaimed by the mouldering ruins of Iona, and by the monuments to the memory of her missionary monks, (the Culdees), found in every neighbouring land. Its records are not only written on the hills and mountains of Wales, and found amidst the sands and on the rocks of Cornwall, but the names of our headlands and harbours, our towns and villages, our sepulchral monuments and churches, unite to confirm the great fact, that even during the fullest triumph of Saxon Paganism in England, Christianity continued to shed its pure and hallowing influence over a large portion of the western part of the island, and was not entirely obliterated, even in the level plains of the eastern counties. And during that time of Britain's woe, when her prelates and their flocks were suffering persecution, and were well-nigh extirpated by the Saxon sword,—who sent forth the noblest of her land, as missionaries and ministers for the protection and maintenance of the Christian faith, amidst those very scenes, but Ireland? Can that fact be now told, and not raise a sigh of pity for their descendants of the present day? Can that fact be now told, and not enkindle a feeling of gratitude and conviction in the heart of every sincere Protestant, that the Lord is now speaking to us, "Freely ye have received the Gospel, freely give." "Go and do thou likewise." Their forefathers rescued many of the sons and daughters of Britain from the chains of Paganism, which the Anglo-Saxons desired to rivet once more on their Christian faith. Can nought be now done by ourselves to repay our debt of gratitude, by uniting in an effort to liberate the natives of our sister isle from the fetters wherewith Popery now holds them bound? Can no young, vigorous sons of England be found to go forth amongst them now, as Protestant missionaries?

With this question we will take our leave of that period of Britain's Church history, which has usually been depicted as lying in the unmitigated darkness of Paganism.

CHAPTER VIII.

Bertha, the Christian Queen of the Anglo-Saxons.—Arrival of Augustine from Rome.—Partial Conversion of the Anglo-Saxons to Christianity, and injudicious Method of extending the Christian Worship amongst them.—Attempt to Subjugate the Ancient British Church to the See of Rome.—Celebrated Interview with Dinoth.—Slaughter of 1,200 Monks at the Battle of Bangor Orchard.—Death of Augustine and Ethelbert.

THE departure of Theanus, Bishop of London, from his see, and his seeking a retreat, with his clergy, and Thadius, Archbishop of York, among the Christians of Wales, was the last historical fact noticed in the foregoing pages; and it was also observed, that it took place only ten years prior to the arrival of Augustine, the celebrated delegate from Gregory of Rome. From authentic history we learn, that at the time of his arrival in the country, henceforth often mentioned as England, many outward circumstances might eventually have effected the conversion of the Anglo-Saxons.* Alford, the Romish Church writer, confesses, that it was very probable, that Imric permitted the Christian religion to be professed in his dominions. And when Augustine appeared, why did he select the spot he did for landing on; but because he knew there then existed a Christian Queen, and a congregation of the same persuasion; worshipping the Lord under the protection

* Columba, if deceased, had only been dead a few months; and the Culdee missionaries were zealously re-establishing Christianity in the north of England, when Augustine arrived.

of her consort, the Bretwalda,* Ethelbert, the son of Imric, and his successor on the throne of Kent.

When this powerful Sovereign had been desirous of marrying the illustrious Princess Bertha, daughter of Charibert, King of Paris, he could only obtain her on condition of her having the full exercise of her own religious belief and worship secured to her. Accordingly, she came hither attended by Luidhard, a Frankish Bishop; and soon the Church of St. Martin,† near Canterbury, was restored, and appropriated to her special use for Divine worship. And therein, writers affirm, Luidhard preached for thirty years. Previous to this time, it is well known that the Anglo-Saxons had applied to the Gallic Churches and their clergy, expressing their desire to have instruction from them, and to receive the Christian faith: evidence in itself, that an overruling Providence, even in that portion of Britain which had suffered most from Saxon wars, had determined that the remembrance of the Christian faith should not be quite obliterated; otherwise the Saxons would never have sought after it. This disposition towards the Christian belief, it is natural to suppose, met with the encouragement of Bertha, their Christian Queen; and doubtless the prayers and piety of herself, Luidhard, and the Christian professors around them, were preparing the King and his subjects for their immediate public reception of the Gospel from Augustine. It is not necessary to enter on the detail of the circumstance which first led to Gregory's taking a peculiar interest respecting the Anglo-Saxons,

---

* Bretwalda, the title enjoyed by the King who had the precedence amongst the other Anglo-Saxon monarchs; a term synonymous with the British one, Pendragon.

† The Church built by, or in the reign of, Lucius.

and induced him, after he became Bishop of Rome, to despatch a Mission to them, because it is so generally recorded in England's secular histories. He appointed Augustine* as the head of his missionary endeavours to effect their conversion in their own land. Other considerations, doubtless, led Gregory to be desirous of extending the Roman See in the West. In that Church, often erroneously held up as an example of unity, he had a powerful rival in John the Faster, who took this opportunity, at Constantinople, for styling himself Œcumenical Bishop. Inconceivably offended, Gregory styled himself "servant of the servants of God," an ostentation of humility ever after retained by the princely pontiffs who have succeeded him, though they have been long unruffled by the Oriental arrogance which then annoyed him. As a counterpoise to the encroaching spirit of his eastern rival, Gregory naturally thought of extending the influence of the Romish See in an opposite direction. Britain presented at this crisis an inviting field for the attempt. Her ancient Church, of true Eastern origin, which, in better days, would probably have spurned any Roman attempt at interference, had been miserably curtailed in the parts subdued by Saxon conquest. An auspicious opening was now offered, by means of their Bretwalda and his Christian spouse, for raising on its ruins a new ecclesiastical establishment. Gregory, well aware of these advantages, judiciously determined upon improving them. This determination is referred by some of our earliest Church historians to an impulse from on high. Nor is this unreasonable: Divine Providence undoubtedly often acts upon the minds of men by outward circumstances, and so orders their affairs as shall most further His own merciful designs.

* Originally a monk in the Convent of St. Andrew, at Rome.

It was not likely that the *political* motives for Gregory's otherwise generous enterprise should be brought into notice by those writers who deeply venerated the See of Rome. The Christian faith had there already become darkened and impeded by the existence and prevalent operation of four great errors:—ascetic doctrines and practices; idolatrous veneration for saints and martyrs; superstitious regard for the sacraments; and the possession and exercise of extravagant despotic powers by the superior clergy. Other details might be added, such as undue reliance on tradition, &c., which would cast increasing gloom upon the picture; but these four leading errors will prepare us for appreciating the character of the religion which the Roman missionaries taught our Saxon ancestors. It must not, however, be supposed, because these Popish errors were so early received by that Church, that all her subsequent errors had been *then* introduced. On the contrary, the doctrine of merit, the greatest practical perversion of Divine grace, was then unknown. Priestly despotism was not then consecrated in the person of one universal Bishop, or Pope. So far from this being the case, Gregory himself declared, that the person who should claim the title of Universal Bishop would be evidently Antichrist. Neither had the clergy of that Church then claimed for her infallibility. Her religious services were also then conducted in the vernacular language of the people, and not, as in following ages, locked up in the darkness of an unknown tongue; neither were the Scriptures wholly withheld from the people. We may, therefore, charitably hope, that even amidst all these errors and superstitions, which certainly choked the growth of pure, vital, and Evangelical religion, there were some who walked in the light of the Divine countenance, and rejoiced in God their Saviour as their only Mediator.

Gregory was a prelate possessed of a most benevolent heart, and one who seems to have deeply lamented the spiritual destitution of his fellow-men, and to have also laboured with zealous energy for the promotion of their evangelization. In him we also find a prelate who valued the Bible, and who even urgently recommended the laity to study it, but who held, notwithstanding, very low and imperfect views of Gospel doctrines and privileges; for, in his recorded replies to inquiries respecting the forgiveness of sins, he appears to have been evidently ignorant of the great doctrine of justification by faith, and of the witness of the Spirit; and the existence of this ignorance accounts most readily for the partiality he manifested for rites and ceremonies. The Mission he destined for the conversion of the Anglo-Saxons halted for a time at Lerins, and from that place they petitioned Gregory to release them from it; but he commanded them to proceed, desiring Augustine, who headed them, to rely on God's protection and support. [A.D. 597.] Augustine, rallying his spirits, accordingly proceeded northwards, and providing himself with interpreters in Gaul, set sail for the chalky cliffs of Kent. He landed in the Isle of Thanet, and thence despatched a messenger to Ethelbert, informing him of his arrival, and declaring that he had journeyed thus far from home in the hope of shewing him the way to everlasting happiness. By the Kentish prince, however well the message might have pleased him, it was cautiously received. He gave no permission to his Roman visitors for their advance into the country, until he had gone himself to make observations. Augustine's arrangements for this Royal visit did honour to his knowledge of human nature. Forming a procession of his monks, one of whom bore a silver cross, another a picture of the Saviour, while the remainder chanted Litanies, he came forward into the presence of the Bretwalda and his Christian Queen. Ethelbert might really have felt fears of magic: none, probably, around him were above such apprehensions; for the reception had been arranged to take place in the open air, magic arts being there considered less likely to take effect. The Prior disclaimed any other object than to guide the King and all his people to everlasting joys above. These were the privileges of his ministry to promise on conversion. "Fair words and promises," Ethelbert replied, "but still new and uncertain. I cannot relinquish for them what my countrymen have long and universally professed. Your distant pilgrimage, however, and charitable purpose of offering us a boon so highly valued by yourselves, justly demand our hospitality. I shall therefore provide you with a residence and means of living. Nor do I restrain you from endeavours to spread your opinions amongst my people."

The residence provided was at Canterbury, and the missionaries entered that city to take possession of it with all those imposing solemnities of the cross, the picture, and the chanted Litany, which had dignified their introduction to the Bretwalda. Of their success there are abundant assurances. Ethelbert, probably long a concealed Christian, seems speedily to have openly professed himself a convert. Nor could his example fail of operating extensively upon the people. Augustine appears, ere long, to have crossed over into Gaul, and to have advised with Virgilius, Archbishop of Arles, upon a public appearance as a Metropolitan of the English nation; and by him was consecrated Archbishop of England. On his return into Kent, he therefore sent Laurence, a priest, and Peter, a monk, with news of his success to Rome. These messengers were, it seems, to give accounts of miracles wrought by Augustine in confirmation and furtherance of his mission. Augustine appears to have been sufficiently forward in thus amusing the semi-barbarous race of his adopted countrymen and converts: probably he lulled his conscience, when he found it convenient, under a little pious fraud (as language poisonously runs), by that false and execrable maxim of Romanists and their disciples, that the end justifies the means.

Gregory's disposition for scrutiny was, unhappily, equally dormant. Apparently his mind was enamoured of the marvellous, and accordingly he appears to have heard of Augustine's miracles with all that implicit credulity which was generally prevalent when the leaden age had once set in. At all events, his political views and habits made him patronise any wonderful tale which seemed likely to raise the dignity and power of the Romish See. Gregory provided also the seeds of future debasements to the Church he had so properly established, by consigning to her new prelate, Augustine, various relics,—the false, frivolous, and disgusting incentives to a grovelling superstition. He likewise transmitted such vestments as appeared to him proper for celebrating the Divine offices; and with still more commendable care for the rising community of Christians, he added several valuable books. Gregory the Great, therefore, not only claims the honour of having embraced a most favourable opportunity for delivering England from Saxon Paganism, but also of having laid the foundation of her literature, by presenting her with the first contributions towards the formation of a library, and her Liturgy.*

In Gregory's "Instructions to Augustine" he seems, in some respects, to have viewed the British and Gallic Churches with a proper feeling and respect, directing him to naturalize in England such usages, whether Roman, Gallic, or other, as might seem best adapted to the feelings and edification of his converts. He sanctioned his single consecration of bishops, if distance prevented his obtaining the assistance of more prelates. Augustine, however, at the same time received from Gregory the insidious compliment of a pall, a sort of cloak, or long robe, worn only by Archbishops, and which raised him to the dignity of Metropolitan over the Anglo-Saxon Church. He charged him also to establish twelve suffragan bishops, and to appoint an Archbishop over the See of York,† over whom he gave him a personal grant of precedence; but after his death the two Archbishops were to rank according to priority of consecration. Augustine's views were immediately directed to the consolidation and extension of his own authority. He invested with Episcopal dignity two ministers, named Mellitus and Justus, and sent them to the kingdom of Essex, where Ethelbert's nephew, Sabert, was reigning, and where Ethelbert (to whom this inferior state was subject) had begun the erection of St. Paul's Church at London, the metropolis of Essex.

On the first indication of Augustine's mission to the Anglo-Saxons being responded to by them, Gregory

* See Appendix, No. II.

† It was already the see of a British or native Archbishop, who might have been summoned from Wales and protected, but the aim was to destroy the British Church, which, being of true Eastern origin, was disliked by Gregory.

had directed that the idol temples should be destroyed. [A.D. June, 601.] Unwisely and unhappily he subsequently rescinded this wholesome order, and wrote: "Let these places of heathen worship be sprinkled with holy water; let altars be built, and relics placed under them; for if these temples are well built, it is fit that the property of them should be altered;* that the worship of devils should be abolished, and the solemnity changed to the service of the true God, in order that when the natives perceive those religious structures remain standing, they may keep to the place without retaining the error, and be less shocked at their first entrance upon Christianity, by frequenting the temples they had been used to esteem. And since it has been their custom to sacrifice oxen to the devils they adored, this usage ought to be refined on † and

---

* Consequently, about A.D. 630, we read that Redwald, King of the East Angles, introduced a table for the Sacrament of Christ into the same temple as contained his idol-god; and as the idols were always placed so as to face the west, and their worshippers had, therefore, to face the east, the similar, and yet unexplained practice of some Christian congregations, of occasionally turning to the east, may thus have been introduced into our worship of the Omnipresent Jehovah. The only mention in the holy Scriptures of turning to the east is in Ezek. viii. 15, forming a most significant condemnation of what the prophet saw in his vision, "O Son of man, turn thee yet again, and thou shalt see greater abominations than these. And he brought me into the inner court of the Lord's house, and behold, at the door of the temple of the Lord, between the porch and the altar, were about five-and-twenty men, with their backs toward the temple of the Lord, and their faces toward the east; and they worshipped the sun toward the east." Scripture nowhere notices the east in connexion with divine worship.

† Previous, however, to these times, we find the apostate Julian reproaching the Christians at Rome with similar practices. And Theodoret, as early as A.D. 423, thus writes to them respecting their care of the relics of saints and martyrs: "For our Lord hath

altered to an 'innocent practice;' and accordingly he further advises, that upon the anniversary of the saints,* whose relics are lodged there, or upon the return of the day on which the church was consecrated, the people should make themselves booths about those churches lately rescued from idolatry, provide an entertainment, and keep a Christian holiday; not sacrificing their cattle to the devil, but killing them for their own refreshment, and praising God for the blessing."

As Archbishop of England, Augustine's views were now directed to the consolidation and extension of his own authority, by endeavouring to subject the British Christians to the Roman See. The influence of Ethelbert was used in bringing the parties together, and Augustine declared his principal object to be no other than to secure British co-operation in the great work of converting the Saxons. The place rendered memorable by this meeting seems to have been under the shade of a noble tree, afterwards known as Augustine's Oak, situated somewhere, probably, on the borders of the Severn, †

---

brought his dead into the place of your gods, whom he hath utterly abolished, and hath given their honour to the martyrs: for, instead of the feasts of Jupiter and Bacchus, are now celebrated the festivals of Peter, and Paul, and Thomas, and the other martyrs.

* To this unscriptural and unwise advice, antiquaries attribute the origin of our parish feasts and fairs; for these assemblings of the people greatly tended to the increase of riot, excess, and every other vice; and as the evil was an attendant following the consecration of every church, an annual provocative to rustic revelry has marked its progress throughout the land for 1,200 years, maintaining an unchanged character to the present time.

† At, or near, Aust, in Gloucestershire, the usual ferry over the Severn into Wales.

in some part of Worcestershire or Gloucestershire. [A.D. 603.]

Augustine, however, then declared that he desired a complete uniformity in religious usages and submission to his authority. The British Church, being of pure Eastern origin, still adhered to a very ancient mode in fixing the festival of Easter, and varied in many other particulars from Roman practice, more, it seems, than in doctrinal opinions. This, however, would not satisfy Augustine. The native Christians were equally intractable, clinging, with fond affection, to those peculiarities of their national Church which bespoke its high antiquity, and which seem, in fact, to connect it immediately with Asia, the cradle of the Christian faith. They accordingly answered most pertinently, when they replied, " that they would do none of these things, nor receive him as their Archbishop."

Argument having failed, Augustine had recourse to one of his miracles. The Britons are said to have "unwillingly consented" to this mode of settling the dispute. A blind man, a Saxon, was then produced, whom the British bishops could not cure, but who, it is said, was immediately restored to sight by Augustine. This miracle, although insufficient to convince the Britons, produced a considerable effect on the bystanders. The only result of this debate was a promise of the Britons, that they would consult the great body of their brethren, and attend another and larger assembly, when it should be convened.

At this second conference, seven British bishops attended, accompanied by the famous Dinoth,* Abbot

* Called by Welsh authors, Dunawd Fawr, and Dunawd Wr.

of the monastery of Bangor, with several learned divines from the same place. Dinoth was the founder of that monastery, and was distinguished for piety and learning, and was then of an advanced age.

In their way, they consulted a hermit, highly esteemed for prudence and holiness. "If Augustine," said the recluse, "be a man of God, take his advice." They then urged the difficulty of ascertaining whether he might be such a man or no. "This is not so difficult," they were told. "Our Lord enjoined, 'Take my yoke upon you and learn of me, for I am meek and lowly in heart.' Now manage to be at the place of meeting after the foreigner, and if he shall rise at your approach, then you may think him to have learnt of Christ; if he should receive you sitting, and show any haughtiness, then maintain your ancient usages." They obeyed his advice.

As the ears of Augustine yet tingled with applause, extorted by admiration of the late miracle on the blind Saxon, no test could have been more unfortunate for him than the one proposed. He arrived at the place of conference, says Archbishop Parker, with the standard of his apostleship,—a silver cross, and various appendages peculiar to the Roman ceremonial; the Litany and Canticles being also sung in procession. The Britons, on their arrival, found Augustine seated in his chair. His address to them was to this effect: "Seeing that in many things ye act contrary to our custom, and even to that of the Universal Church, yet if ye will obey me in three points—that ye celebrate Easter at its proper time; that ye complete the service of Baptism (by

The Latin name is Dinothus, and Bede, the Saxon Romanist, calls him, Dinoot Abbas.

which we are born again unto God) after the manner of the holy Roman Catholic Church; and, that ye preach the word of God, in conjunction with us, to the Anglo-Saxons,—all other things which ye do, although contrary to our customs, we will bear them all with patience."

Dinoth, in the name of his brethren, entered at large, with great gravity and learning, on the subjects of difference between the two Churches, the issue being thus handed down to us: "We agree to no one of your propositions; much less can we admit as our Archbishop, one, who will not even rise to salute us. Besides, we are under the government of the Bishop of Caerleon,* who is, under God, appointed to superintend us, and to cause us to continue in the spiritual way." Dinoth further argued on the impropriety of receiving the authority of Augustine, and defended the jurisdiction of their own primate, and affirmed it not to be for the British interest to own either Roman pride or Saxon tyranny.

Augustine now seeing himself completely foiled, became enraged, and hastily said, "If they would not accept peace from their brethren, they must expect war from their enemies; and if they would not preach the Word of Life to the Saxons, they should suffer death at their hands."

Not many years after this declaration, 1,200 of the monks of Dinoth's celebrated monastery at Bangor were slain unarmed on the field of battle, near Chester, by the Anglo-Saxon King, Ethelfrid. Whether Au-

* The primacy of Wales was of a very migratory character, the see being sometimes at St. David's, and sometimes at Caerleon: and so it continued for six hundred years after this conference.

gustine's threat was uttered as a random prophecy, or in the spirit of meditated revenge, is a point not yet settled by historians. It is known only to Him who searcheth the heart, and alone knows what is in the heart of man. Augustine died a few years after this conference. Writers differ whether it took place before the already alluded to celebrated battle of the Orchard of Bangor, or after. The Saxons were led on by Ethelfrid, the pagan King of Northumberland, who, having taken Chester, advanced into Wales. The monks of Bangor, remembering the threats of Augustine, were filled with alarm, but they accompanied the British soldiers to the field of battle. The King, observing them apart, (for they were engaged in earnest prayer to God,) thus commanded that they should be first attacked: "Who are all these unarmed men?" asked this Anglican chief. "Monks," was the reply, "brought hither, after a three days' fast, to pray for success upon their country's arms." Ethelfrid rejoined, "They are active enemies no less than the others; for they come to fight against us with their prayers. First put them to the sword." Bede, who acknowledges the fact, and knew that the Saxons, who had destroyed them, were heathens, yet speaks of the Britons as "a perfidious nation," an impious army, "perfidious men," and attributes the circumstance to the Divine judgment. Bede, let it be borne in mind, was a Saxon and a Romanist, and his treatment of the subject seems to indicate, that if Augustine had not directly, or indirectly, prompted the Saxons to this cause of aggression and slaughter, the Anglo-Saxon Christians regarded the deed rather with pleasure than otherwise.

The noble monastery of Bangor, after this murder of

1,200 of its monks, fell into the hands of the enemy, was levelled to the ground by Ethelfrid, and never after raised its head. This slaughter must sadly have thinned the leading ranks of British Christians, yet they retained sufficient spirit and prowess to vindicate their honour; and by whomsoever this sanguinary invasion into their territories had been instigated, it was promptly and effectually repelled and chastised; for under the command of Blederich, Duke of Cornwall, the Britons marched to attack the invaders on the banks of the Dee. Here the Anglo-Saxon army was routed with the loss of 10,060 killed: and Ethelfrid, being wounded, was obliged to stipulate that he would retreat within his own country, north of Trent, and leave all Wales to be entirely and peaceably enjoyed by the Britons. Soon after, if not just before, this invasion, Augustine, the pioneer in the conversion of the Anglo-Saxons, as before noticed, died. As well as Gregory, he deserves our gratitude and veneration. Gregory's conduct, though he was evidently too much attached to the See of Rome, appears a shining light of missionary zeal. Had he contemplated the subsequent apostasy of his favourite Church,* probably he would not have sanctioned the introduction of many of those practices admitted into the Christian worship by Augustine. The stain of rivalry and jealousy which

* The following are the *periods* when the principal Popish errors were, subsequent to Gregory's time, made articles of faith, by the sanction of what was called a General Council:—

	A.D.		A.D.
Invocation of Saints	700	Half Communion	1415
Image Worship	787	Purgatory	1438
Infallibility	1076	Seven Sacraments	1547
Transubstantiation	1215	Sacrifice of the Mass	1563
Supremacy	1215		

appeared in their conduct towards other Churches, must be forgiven—they were but men. Moreover, the ambitious spirit of encroachment manifested towards the Primitive British Church must be laid on Augustine, whose object appears to have been self-aggrandizement, being also led on by the superstition of the age and an excessive zeal of conformity, to attempt to subdue or extirpate that Church. Augustine was soon followed to the tomb by his friend and protector, Ethelbert, King of Kent and Bretwalda, A.D. 616. As a statesman, he was great; as a Christian, greater still; and few princes, in any age, were richer blessings to their subjects than Ethelbert and Bertha.

CHAPTER IX.

Relapse of Anglo-Saxons to Paganism.—Laurentius Eadbald.—Conversion of Edwin and his Followers in Northumbria to Christianity.—Paulinus. — Subsequent Relapse. — Northumbria finally converted from Paganism by Aiden and Finan.—Coleman.—Wilfrid.—Council of Whitby.—Theodore.

AUGUSTINE was succeeded, as Archbishop of Canterbury, by Laurentius; but the promising aspect which the Christian cause maintained at the death of Ethelbert was soon obscured by a dark cloud; for his son and successor, Eadbald, renounced the profession of Christianity; and Sebert, King of Essex, dying soon after, his sons relapsed likewise into idolatry, and forbad the return of Mellitus, who had long been absent at Rome, but appeared in time to consult with Laurentius and Justus, when they all determined to leave the country. This purpose Mellitus and Justus immediately put into execution, and sailed over to France, while Laurentius remained behind for a few days. For the purpose of working on the feelings or conscience of Eadbald, who he knew had been bred and educated a Christian, the Archbishop, the night previous to his departure, resorted to one of those pious frauds, of which, in those days, when religion appeared in a kind of transition-state (if we may so speak), passing from primitive purity to Popish darkness and superstition, ministers of the Gospel, it is grievous to have to record, were found too often availing themselves of. Milner does not mention the circumstance in the text of his work, but in a note observes, " I was unwilling to introduce into the narrative the story of St. Peter's whipping of Laurentius that night in the church, and reproving him for his cowardice ; whence he was said to have been induced to wait upon Eadbald next morning, who was struck, it seems, with remorse at the sight of the stripes which the Bishop had received." An ingenious fraud being thus resorted to, an actual falsehood was told (if the story has reached us correctly), to forward the purposes of Laurentius. What an awful amount of darkness must have gathered over the first principles of Christianity in the Romish Church at that date, before a learned and serious mind, with a good intention, could have sunk into such unworthy means of promoting a holy cause! The efforts of Laurentius were partially successful. Eadbald repented and amended, and Christianity was again acknowledged in Kent.* [A. D. 624.] Mellitus ventured to return, but the inhabitants of London refusing him admittance there, he retired to Canterbury, where he remained ; and on the decease of Laurentius, he succeeded him as Archbishop. About this period, the Gospel triumphed, for a time, over Saxon Heathenism in Northumbria. Romantic and interesting tales are attached to the circumstances of its introduction in those parts ; but the substance appears to be, that Edwin, the rightful heir to the throne, after years of adventure, at length became firmly seated thereon, and solicited in marriage the

* In Kent, Eadbald was eventually succeeded by his son, Eascoubert, who, for twenty-four years, zealously supported the cause of godliness, and was the first Saxon King who totally destroyed all the idols in his kingdom.

hand of Ethelburga, sister of Eadbald, King of Kent, and only obtained his suit by consenting to allow her and her attendants the free exercise of the Christian religion, and of turning his own serious attention to the nature and evidences of this holy faith. This Christian lady, the daughter of Queen Bertha, under whose auspices Christianity had been first introduced amongst the Saxons of Kent, took with her Paulinus, who, on this occasion, was consecrated Archbishop of York. [A.D. 625.] Paulinus laboured in Northumbria for a year without success. At the end of this period, Edwin had a very narrow escape from the assault of an assassin, who had been sent to destroy him by Quickhlenc, King of the West Saxons: he was wounded, and one of his courtiers slain. On the same day, his Christian Queen, Ethelburga, gave birth to a daughter, and Paulinus at once returned thanks for both mercies. Edwin assured Paulinus that he would renounce idolatry and serve Christ entirely, if God would preserve his life and give him victory over his perfidious enemies. As a pledge, he gave his infant daughter to Paulinus, that she might be consecrated to Christ in baptism. This infant princess was the first of the Saxon Northumbrians that was baptized; with her, twelve others of her family partook of the same rite. Edwin sought and defeated his enemies; and the Queen and Paulinus then united their entreaties that he would, according to his promise, embrace Christianity. The King hesitated, but summoned his Barons to a Witana-gemot,* that the subject of the

---

* The Parliament, or Legislative Assembly of the nation under the Anglo-Saxon Kings, was called the Witana-gemot. On every such meeting of the great National Council, Anglo-Saxon Archbishops, Bishops, and Abbots were provided with their appropriate

new worship might be discussed. Coifi, the high priest, who presided over the idol worship, delivered his sentiments in a remarkable style, self-interest and a conviction of the declining influence of Paganism being easily detected as the true essence of his speech. That of the next speaker, a Thane, or Earlderman, is still more remarkable and interesting, and was to this effect:—" The life of man, O King, reminds me of a winter feast around your blazing fire. While the storm howls, or the snow drives abroad, a distressed sparrow darts within the doorway; for a moment is cheered, by warmth and shelter, from the blast; then, shooting through the other entrance, it is lost again. Such is man! He comes, we know not whence, hastily snatches a scanty share of worldly pleasures, then goes we know not whither. If this new doctrine, therefore, will give us any clearer insight into things of so much interest, my feeling is to follow it."

Before such arguments, strikingly resembling those of Indian warriors in America, Northumbrian Paganism fell. Coifi was foremost in making war upon the superstition which had so severely baulked his hopes. His priestly character obliged him to ride a mare, and forbad him to bear a weapon. The people, therefore, thought him mad, when he appeared on

places. Thus the civil polity of England was wisely founded on a Christian basis. The clerical estate has formed an integral member of it from the first. An English prelate's right to occupy the legislative seat that has descended to him from a long line of his predecessors, is, therefore, founded on the most venerable of national prescriptions. It is no privilege derived from Norman polity which converted Episcopal endowments into baronies. It is far more ancient than the Conqueror's time, being rooted amidst the very foundation of the *more* ancient monarchy.

Edwin's charger, lance in hand. He rode forthwith to a famous temple at Godmundham, in Yorkshire, pierced the idol through, and ordered the building to be burnt. Soon afterwards, Paulinus kept Easter at York, holding a public baptism; Edwin, his principal men, and multitudes of the inferior people, being then likewise solemnly admitted into the outward Christian Church. [A.D. 627.] Paulinus was ostensibly established at York as his Episcopal see. His mission, however, eventually failed. His patron, Edwin, fell in battle; frightful destruction followed; and Northumbria so completely relapsed into Paganism, that Ethelburga, the Queen, attended by Paulinus, sought safety on shipboard, and sailed into Kent.

In estimating the nature and extent of the labours of Paulinus we must not be misled by the term Bishop or Archbishop; for when he and the Court arrived from Kent he brought no clergy with him; and when he fled, on the death of Edwin, from the scene of his labours, no mention is made of any ministers he took with him or left behind him, with the exception of James, a deacon, who remained at York, where a faithful remnant of Christians was preserved through his individual ministry. Paulinus always appears on the page of history, in the character more of a chaplain or preacher to the King and Royal family, with whom he always moved, than as a prelate; but, like the primitive apostles, he officiated as a field preacher, ministering and baptizing frequently on the banks of rivers. Though he baptized multitudes in a day on some grand occasions, the personal experience of vital godliness, it is to be feared, was limited to very few individuals; for, on his departure, Northumberland, for a time, sank again, as we have stated, into Saxon Paganism.

[A.D. 633.] During a short period this country became the theatre of a barbarous and desolating war, but, eventually, Oswald, a nephew of the late Bretwalda, Edwin, was settled on the throne of Northumberland. This prince, whilst an exile, had been converted to the faith of Christ amongst the Irish, and being no admirer of Roman innovations, he sent to Iona for a Culdee Bishop to instruct his people in Evangelical truth. In consequence of which, Aiden, an Irishman, and a Culdee of Iona, was there consecrated and sent over to him. The King gave the Bishop the isle of Lindisfarne, or Holy Isle, on the coast of Northumberland, for his episcopal see. He would not accept the See of York, as the Culdees, in imitation of their master, Columba, preferred islands; and, secondly, he considered, though originally a British episcopate, as it had been selected by Gregory as a see, it might be regarded as an acquiescence in the decision of that Roman Pontiff, to which the Irish hierarchy, complete and independent in itself, had not submitted. Oswald personally attended Aiden's ministry; and when the latter preached, as he did not perfectly understand the Anglo-Saxon language, the King was his interpreter,* for during Oswald's exile in Ireland he had learnt the language of the island. Numbers of Culdees daily arrived at this time from Ireland; those who were priests baptized the converted. Aiden built a church and founded a monastery at Lindisfarne, where he acted as bishop, abbot, and teacher in Divinity; and from thence he sent forth numerous preachers as missionaries into the neighbouring provinces; Aiden was likewise a luminous example of charity, piety, and abstinence,

* Thus he was styled the King-interpreter.

and recommended his doctrine by his practice. The happy results of these efforts of a pious King and bishops, assisted by the Scotch and Irish clergy, were soon perceived; for the cause and abiding influence of religion greatly progressed in this part of the country. Aiden died in 651, and was succeeded by Finan, an Irishman and Culdee of Iona. King Oswald, in the thirty-eighth year of his age, was slain in battle by Penda, King of Mercia—a memorable instance of the unsearchable ways of Providence; for he and Edwin, two kings of Northumberland, whose equals in piety and virtue could not easily be found in any age, both lost their lives in battle with the same enemy,—Penda, a barbarian and a Pagan.

According to Bede, Finan was "a man of rough and fierce nature, but was very successful in his ministerial labours, and not only converted and baptized Peada, king of the Middle Angles, along with all his Court, but sent four priests to instruct his subjects in Christianity. Sigbert, King of the East Angles, was also baptized by him, as well as his people; and he sent for two other bishops, to assist him in the ministry of ordination, and consecrated Cedda, or Chad, Bishop of the East Angles." Romanists boast of the great success of Augustine in converting the Saxons to Christianity, but the principal merit of their conversion is due to the zealous labours of Irish missionaries. In justice to them, Archbishop Usher observes, "St. Aiden and St. Finan deserve to be honoured by the English nation with as venerable a remembrance as Austin, the monk, and his followers."* Whilst

* According to the Archbishop's account, by the ministry of Aiden, besides the shire of Northumberland, the lands beyond it, to Edinburgh, Firth, Cumberland, Westmoreland, Lancashire,

Christianity was thus becoming firmly rooted in the northern and midland parts of England by the pious endeavours of these exemplary bishops, it was gradually gaining on the prejudices of other heathen Angles. Birinus, a priest of Rome, was despatched [A.D. 635] from thence to preach the Gospel in the north of Britain, but landing among the West Saxons, and finding them entirely heathens, he turned his attention to them.

In thus carefully studying the progress of Christianity at this period, it is satisfactorily proved, that only two counties north of the Thames were ever under Roman superintendence during their transition from Paganism to Christianity, and these were Norfolk and Suffolk; every other county from London to Edinburgh, has the full gratification of pointing to the ancient Church of Britain as its nursing mother in Christ's holy faith. The West Saxons were chiefly converted by means of the above-named Birinus, the Roman monk; and his labours probably owed a large portion of their success to Oswald, (our already-mentioned King of Northumberland) who, at the same time as himself, arrived at the West Saxon Court, as a suitor to the King's daughter. At such a time it was found an easy matter to convert the young princess and her father, Kynegils. To the latter Oswald stood sponsor, nor did he leave the south with his bride until he had

Yorkshire, and Durham, were effectually recovered from Saxon Paganism. And to the means of Finan, also a Culdee Bishop, Usher attributes the same blessing in respect to Essex, Middlesex, and half of Hertfordshire, Gloucestershire, Leicestershire, Worcestershire, Northamptonshire, Lincolnshire, Huntingdonshire, Bedfordshire, Buckinghamshire, Oxfordshire, Staffordshire, Derbyshire, Shropshire, Nottinghamshire, and part of Herefordshire. So little did God bless the labours of the boasted apostle of England!

accomplished arrangements for providing Birinus with an episcopal see at Dorchester, in Oxfordshire. Thus, even the West Saxon Church was importantly indebted to a powerful and kingly professor of the ancient national Church, for its firm establishment.

[A. D. 640.] The Bishop who succeeded Birinus was Agilbert, a Frenchman, who had long studied in Ireland, and who undertook an especial mission to the West Saxons, by desire of Oswy, King of Northumberland. The Gospel, having thus won its way over other parts of England, at length obtained an establishment in Sussex. Ædilwach, King of Sussex, whilst on a visit to the King of Mercia, was converted, and returned to his own country a Christian. His people, however, seem to have been chiefly indebted to the famous Wilfrid, then a wanderer, and a zealous partisan of Rome, for their conversion. In Sussex, therefore, the cases of Essex and Northumbria were reversed. In these latter counties, a Roman introduction through Paulinus and a queen prepared the way for the success of British bishops and missionaries. Among the South Saxons, British kings and clergy made an opening through which Rome prevailed. Her complete and final prevalence over the ancient national Church, existing from the apostolic age, flowed from female influence and the intriguing dexterity of her agents, who, gradually assimilating the services of the Church and its rites to the Romish Church, thereby paved the way for the introduction of its unscriptural doctrines and domineering influence over the nation, both in Church and State.

[A. D. 661.] Finan, the worthy successor of Aiden in the northern see of Lindisfarne, when he died, was succeeded therein by Coleman, a Culdee of Iona, who was an intrepid opposer of Papal doctrine, practices, and assumptions; but he does not appear to have been possessed of the same ability as his predecessors. This was seized on by the Romanist party for effecting their insidious purposes, and *accordingly a violent controversy was agitated by them* regarding some points in which the ancient national Church differed from the Romish, especially those respecting Easter and the tonsure. It is humiliating to be obliged to confess, that such were the two points selected by the Romishly-inclined Anglo-Saxon clergy, to effect the submission of the ancient Church to the See of Rome. Hitherto the native clergy had offered the greatest obstacle to the accomplishment of that purpose, though they did not at all interfere with the usages or regulations introduced by the clergy of the Romish communion, and left them at liberty to hold their sacred festivals and to follow the rites of their own Church. This was not sufficient. The Romish priests, not satisfied with toleration, claimed superiority and submission. The claim, however, was not put forth specifically and formally; but the two points already mentioned were selected for the purpose of insidiously enforcing a conformity to the customs and practice of Rome, in order thus to prepare the way for the universal establishment of her authority. The Romish party likewise instigated the Queen to disquiet the King, who being thus tampered with, at length convened a Synod to meet at Whitby, where he appeared in anything but the character of an efficient or impartial arbitrator.

[A.D. 664.] At the appointed time Coleman and his clergy, and the lady Hilda, appeared on the part of the ancient Church; and, on the other side, Bishop Agilbert, who had been removed from the See of Dorchester on account of the dissensions he had created, and was then Bishop of Paris. Coleman, however devout, sincere, and intrepid a Christian, was not a match for the wily Wilfrid, who was present, and seeking to press forward the Romish interest as the most likely means of furthering his own selfish and ambitious views; yet it proved a thorny and perplexing path to honour and renown. This extraordinary man, destined to effect such momentous changes in the Saxon Church, had very early in life forsaken his father's roof to escape domestic disquiet, and had contrived to find his way to the Northumbrian Court, where, observing Queen Eanfleda's partiality to the Romish Church, he determined to gratify his own inclination and push his own interest by espousing its cause. Accordingly, bearing recommendations from his queenly patroness, he travelled to Rome, where he abode for some months, learnt the four Gospels, as also the Easter calculation, unknown to the schismatics (as they were called at Rome) of Britain and Ireland; and also the exact cut of the tonsure of St. Peter; when he returned home, and was placed, by the contrivance of the Queen, as tutor to the young prince. Such was Wilfrid, Abbot of Ripon, whom, on this memorable occasion, Agilbert, the ex-Bishop, introduced on the platform of religious controversy, in the presence of two kings, several bishops, presbyters, and other clerks and spectators, composed of Britons, Scots, Picts, Romans, Angles, and Saxons. Interesting as the whole detail of the conference might be, the present is by far too unpretending a volume to sanction more intrusion on the time of the young reader, than to state, that the Northumbrian King opened it in a speech dwelling on the importance of unity in the Church, and calling on Coleman to state his views respecting the observance of Easter. Coleman rested the correctness of their computation on that "which," said he, "I have received from my elders, and it is the same as St. John, the Evangelist, observed, with all the Churches over which he presided." * Wilfrid argued in favour of the Romish calculation, which he summed up by stating "it had been derived from St. Peter, who held the keys of heaven, which had been given him by the Lord." Whereupon the King decided in favour of the Roman party; "for," said he, "St. Peter is a door-keeper whom I am unwilling to contradict. I should not like to disoblige him who keeps the keys of heaven. It might be found impossible to get the door open when I seek admittance."

Unless one again remembered the chieftains of America, this language would seem like jest, rather than as spoken in earnest. But it was generally applauded, and the ancient usages of Britain sank beneath it, and yielded acquiescence to the pretended ordinances of St. Peter. The Roman party had gained their point by establishing the first encroaching step on the liberty of the Church of Christ in England, and they had only insidiously still further to carry on the work; for, the outward triumph *now* gained involved little or no change in doctrines.

Coleman, when he found his opinions set aside, resigned his see, rather than submit to such a decision: thus furnishing the historian with a remarkable proof that the Irish, as well as the Scotch and British Churches, in the seventh century, still rejected the

* See page 23.

authority of the bishops of Rome. He collected all the Irish Culdees at Lindisfarne, and, with some English monks, resorted for a time to Iona, and at last sailed for Ireland, where he spent the remaining part of his life, in the island of the White Cow, called in Irish, Inis-bo-fin. He also built and founded the monastery of Magio, (now Mayo,) with the assistance of the Earl of that place, for the accommodation of the English, who there lived under canonical rule, and an abbot, in great tranquillity, supporting themselves by the labour of their own hands.

Immediately on the departure of Coleman, the Culdees were everywhere expelled from England by Oswy, and replaced by Benedictines. Although at this time the Saxon kingdoms had gradually and completely fallen into ecclesiastical bondage, the remains of the ancient British Churches struggled zealously and perseveringly against this unrighteous domination. Soon after this Synod, Cedd, or Chad, who had succeeded Coleman in his see, was carried off by a pestilence which then prevailed.

The effects were now to be exhibited which resulted from the virtual recognition of Romish supremacy, that had been granted at the Council of Whitby; for when the death of Cead, the successor of Chad, gave Wilfrid promotion to the Episcopate, he disregarded the consecration to be obtained at Canterbury, crossed the sea, and received it from his early patron, Agilbert, Bishop of Paris. He did not then return to the duties of his see, but lingered on his way to display his new dignity amongst the tempting hospitalities of Gaul. His Royal patron in England, disgusted with this, bestowed the bishopric upon Cead, brother to the deceased Cedd, or Chad. The Archbishop of Canterbury died before he could consecrate him, but Cead repaired to Winchester, where the ceremony was performed by Wine, the Prelate, and two British bishops. This was the tangible opportunity for raising another religious commotion, and the Saxon kings, hoping to quell the same, sent a worthy man for consecration as Primate to Rome, but there he died. The opportunity afforded by his death at Rome was not lost by Italian subtlety. Vitilian, then Pope, or Bishop, determined upon trying if the Anglo-Saxons would receive an Archbishop of his nomination. He chose eventually Theodore, a learned and able monk, and a native of Tarsus, in Cilicia. The Saxon princes, wearied by the animosities of contending parties, only sought an umpire likely to command respect: hence, they did not merely receive Theodore, but also eventually conceded to him that primacy over the whole Anglo-Saxon Church which had been vainly sought by Augustine.

One of the first causes referred to Theodore was that of Wilfrid and Cead, both having, by consecration, claims to the See of Northumbria. Of course, Theodore, as coming from the See of Rome, decided, that as Cead's consecration had been partly obtained through the assistance of British bishops at the ceremony, it was uncanonical. Cead, a pious and humble man, would gladly have retired entirely; but at length consented to receive consecration from Theodore, and became Bishop of Mercia, and Wilfrid was reinstated in the See of Northumbria.

[A. D. 673.] Theodore convened a national Synod at Hertford, when he produced a selection of canons from those established at Rome. In examining their purposes and tendency under the influence of Christian principles and feelings, we have to regret the secular character they maintain. No allusion is made to the spiritual edification or condition of the Christians, or the best means of promoting their eternal interests. The whole time of the Council was expended in settling matters relative to the honours and privileges of the superior clergy, and enforcing rules adapted to make the inferior clergy dependant on the bishops, and, if found refractory, that they should be disqualified from officiating, and disowned. The only canon introduced which bore the appearance of concern for the spiritual welfare of the Church, by providing an increase of bishops as Christianity progressed amongst the Saxons, was the only one rejected; exhibiting a line of conduct diametrically opposed to that proof of love the Lord Jesus required of Peter, in almost his parting words to him, "Feed my lambs: feed my sheep." The worldly and coercive spirit manifested at this Synod did not secure the submission and unity in the Church which it was intended it should. Theodore, as Metropolitan, still desired to divide the dioceses, (each as co-extensive as the kingdoms of the Heptarchy), and to have more bishops appointed. The spiritual interests of the people required it, and the practice of the apostles and the primitive Churches alike called for such a measure. Yet the Synod refused to confirm his wish, and the celebrated Wilfrid, whose widely-extended diocese Theodore and the King had resolved on dividing, boldly accused them of injustice, and declared that he would appeal to the Bishop of Rome—a threat at that time so new, that it was received with a laugh. Wilfrid, who lived in more than the regal magnificence of those days, being seriously alarmed that he should have to lay it aside, put his threat into execution.

On stating his case at Rome, the Pope acquitted him of "*all charges, certain and uncertain,*" and sent him back with an order that those who had been made sharers in his diocese should be expelled. In open council the King unsealed the Papal document.

The time had not yet arrived when Anglo-Saxon princes obeyed the mandates of the Pope, or Bishop of Rome, or trembled at his frown; for Egfrid, the King, by the advice of his council, sent Wilfrid to prison. At the expiration of a year, the King released him therefrom, upon condition that he quitted his territories. His character being known, he was generally shunned, but at last he sought and obtained refuge in the still Pagan country of Sussex, and was cordially received by the Court, who were well inclined to Christianity; and, as it proved a season of scarcity, he laudably contributed to alleviate the distress by imparting to the natives a profitable mode of fishing; and, through this means, introduced Christianity amongst them. This public service seems to have conciliated the Archbishop, and the King, who had succeeded Egfrid on the throne of Northumberland, permitted him to return to his dominions. He was also granted considerable preferment, but again becoming dissatisfied and turbulent, he was again expelled that kingdom. [A.D. 687.]

Theodore had, during this period, procured a meeting of the Anglo-Saxon clergy at Hatfield, at which were revived the first five General Councils, and the Synod lately holden at Rome. [A.D. 690.] Not long after which, this celebrated Primate died. He was certainly one of the greatest men who ever filled the chair of Canterbury. By his influence, the Anglo-Saxon Churches were brought under an uniform discipline. Bishoprics were divided; prelates again increased; and the foundation of parish churches in England formed; and the clergy thereof provided for, by following the plan adopted in his native Asia. Under Royal sanction, he also induced opulent proprietors to supply the spiritual wants of their tenantry, by offering them the perpetual patronage of such churches as they erected and endowed. But Theodore's oriental system had been in partial operation for ages before, as every Anglo-Saxon estate of any magnitude had already secured the benefit of a church within its boundary. This may account for the isolated situation of many parish churches in rural districts. A Protestant must truly regret that the eminent qualities Theodore possessed were, however, directed to other measures, which laid the foundation of an insidious influence, that furthered the progress of error, adulterated sound religion, and insulted the national independence. Yet it must be owned that he looked on the Papal See with an oriental feeling of independence, and therefore, though he unwittingly became the corner-stone on which Pontifical authority was erected in England, his name will vainly be sought among the saintly rubrics in a Romish calendar! His reputation stands on higher ground!

CHAPTER X.

Wilfrid's turbulent Life.—Christian Biography.—Irish and British Missionaries on the Continent.—Aldhelm.—Bede.—Alcuin.

[A. D. 689.] THEODORE having been led to hope, that a reformation in Wilfrid's turbulent spirit had been effected by adversity, and viewing with approbation his aforementioned endeavours to Christianize and benefit the Pagan population of Sussex, on his death-bed, so far pleaded in his favour to the Court of Northumbria, that Wilfrid was restored to some of his preferments; but he who had risen in adversity, sank in prosperity. Wilfrid's haughty and untractable spirit would not yield submission to the deceased Theodore's canons, &c., and, therefore, under Brithwald, his successor, he was again ejected and expelled the kingdom. Wilfrid, at the age of seventy, again repaired to Rome for redress, and, again obtaining its bishop's approbation, he returned to his native land, where, involving himself anew in religious and political strife, he was once more rebuffed; but at length retired to the Abbey of Ripon, as Bishop of Hexham, and lived peaceably for the last four years of his life. Wilfrid's is the first example which has reached us of appeals to Rome from this country; but history, at the same time, shows that, both ecclesiastically and civilly, they were treated with the utmost contempt by the Anglo-Saxon Church. These appeals, and his indefatigable zeal for Papal usage, were naturally considered by the Romish power as an ample title to its invocation. St. Wilfrid's tutelage was, accordingly, long implored in northern England.

[A.D. 709.] A little anterior to his death, the progress of events had effected much towards the secular settlement of the Anglo-Saxon Church; and it accordingly put on the bearing of a Christian commonwealth. The care which was, about this period, taken to secure the Divine ministrations to the community at large, under the name of "Church shot," with penalties imposed on defaulters, may be regarded as the origin of Church rates. The Anglo-Saxons had been prepared for such demands after conversion, from habits previously * formed; for provision for the ministers of religion had been rendered, in every previous age, to every description of national religion. Hence, the origin of tithes probably ascends to that patriarchal faith, which ever shed a glimmering though distorted ray over the most benighted branches of Adam's wandering posterity, who were cut off from the direction of Jehovah's written laws.† When Christianity was introduced amongst them, it strengthened Pagan prejudice in favour of this appropriation; and accordingly, the Anglo-Saxons seem to have here found "the tenth," esteemed God's portion among the British Christians.

Turning aside from the immediate detail of religious and political disquietudes, let us now refresh our feelings by taking a retrospective glance over the lives of some of those pious British individuals who lived apart from them; and anterior to, and during the stormy days of, Theodore and Wilfrid.‡

---

* See page 20.—Lucius.   † See page 4.—Japhethites.
‡ Theodore did much for Saxon literature, not only individually,

While Aiden, Finan, Cedda, &c., &c., were labouring in their vocation and calling amongst the Pagan Anglo-Saxons, other natives of the British Isles were as zealously employed in preaching the unsearchable riches of Christianity to the inhabitants of Europe. But before that time a young Irishman, called Fridolin, "the traveller," had been the honoured instrument in God's hands, of bringing the first message of salvation to the Alemanni, of the Upper Rhine. At an early age, having formed the resolution of devoting his life to the missionary cause, he itinerated about Ireland, preaching the Gospel from village to village. Passing over to the Continent, Fridolin there scattered the good seed on the right hand and on the left, and finally settled in a little island, where the small town of Sekingen (between Basle and Schaffhausen) now stands. Having been presented by Clovis to the whole of the island, he built a monastery there; which being resorted to by pious monks, proved the foundation of Christ's Church in the German provinces. Fridolin undertook another mission to the country of the Glarni, but returning to his island, he died there, in the year 538.

Fifty years after the mission of Fridolin, additional light was sent to the Alemanni, through the instrumentality of Columbanus * and twelve companions.

but through the medium of his friend Adrian, a learned African, who acted under the direction of Vitilian, the Pope, in the double capacity of a spy on his actions. This espionage, his successor gladly renewed by means of one known as John the Precentor, introduced, it was said, for the purpose of instructing a community of monks in chanting the service, and reading Latin. Who can fathom the tricks of Popery? None but God.

* It was usually the custom, in the early days of the Church, to give new names to the distinguished servants of Christ, according

Columbanus was a descendant of a noble family in Leinster, and was educated in the monasteries of Iona and Bangor,* in Ulster. He was urged by an irresistible desire to carry forth the name of the Lord into the wide world of Paganism, (A.D. 590,) and hearing a lamentable account of the state of Christianity in Gaul, he first preached, for a considerable time, in that country; but finding a spot suited to the retirement of his taste, and the sanctity of his purpose, in the gloomy and sequestered forest of Upper Burgundy, in the neighbourhood of the Alps, he there built twelve cabins for himself and his companions, most of whom, if not all, were afterwards missionaries in other parts. The noble, the rich, and the poor, all flocked to him for instruction; but at length, reproving the guilty life of the Duke of Burgundy, he had to quit that place. Columbanus, with his zealous companion, Gallus, remained amongst the Pagans, dwelling near Zurich, in Switzerland, and afterwards passed on to an extensive plain near the upper Lake of Constance, where they were well received: progressing through the country, which still lay desolate from the effects of Attila's march, only very few traces of the ancient Christian settlements were found. Within the walls of a ruined

to their supposed or inherent virtues: thus Columba, the dove, and afterwards Columna-cille, which, in Irish, is "the dove of the Church;" and, again, Columbanus, the wild pigeon, or wood-guest.

* The word Bangor is a Welsh one, implying any College: and all Christian societies among the Britons began to assume that epithet towards the close of the fifth century. Before that period, the British Christians called their societies by the simple name of Côr, a circle, or congregation; but at the time above mentioned, they dignified the name by the additional epithet of Ban, high, superior, or supreme—that is to say, Bangor.

Christian Church, which had been used by the Pagans as an idol-temple, the first Christian sermon was preached to the heathen Alemanni of the neighbourhood. A Christian village was built on the spot, and here, for a time, a goodly company of converted Alemanni formed a settlement. The missionaries laid out gardens, planted fruit-trees, and prosecuted their trade as fishermen for food and traffic, on the Lake of Constance, with success: and what is far better, they were eminently successful as fishers of men. After three years' hard labour, Columbanus and some of his disciples had to flee from persecution, and crossed the high Alps into Italy. It was on this occasion that Columbanus founded the monastic seminary named Bobio,* for the education of able missionaries to the heathen Longobards, and lived to see their King, Agilulph, with a number of his subjects, added to the Church. By the advice of this prince, Columbanus addressed a letter of considerable vigour and spirit to Boniface I., Bishop of Rome, who claimed the supremacy, still arrogated to itself by the Papacy. In this interesting epistle Columbanus addresses Boniface in a respectful, and, at the same time, an extraordinary style, but rebukes the *soi-disant* Pope in these terms: " That thou mayest not be deprived of apostolic honour, preserve apostolic faith; confirm it by testimony; strengthen it by writing; fortify it by Synod, that none may justly resist thee. Watch, therefore, I entreat thee, O Pope, watch; and again, I say watch: because haply Vigilius did not carefully keep vigil, whom those who cast blame upon you cry out to be the original cause of the scandal." Bold language this to be addressed, by an humble monk from Ireland, to the

* See page 53.

great and powerful Bishop of Rome: "That thou mayest not lack apostolic honour, preserve the apostolic faith." If the apostolic faith be not preserved, the apostolic honour must fail, and then the time has arrived, when resistance may be right and lawful. This is the obvious meaning of the foregoing language, and this was the very principle, when worked out, that produced the blessed Reformation. Other passages in this letter are still more irreconcileable with the views of Papal supremacy that have gained currency since his time; but we have not space to admit them, however interesting they may be.

In 616 Columbanus was called from his labours, after having, with great self-denial and mortification, consecrated forty-two years of his life to the promulgation of Christianity amongst the inhabitants of France, Germany, and Italy; and having educated and sent forth a great multitude of disciples for the same blessed employment.

When Columbanus crossed the Alps, he left at the hut of the pious Willimar (who had first received him and his followers) the most distinguished one amongst them, Gallus, who was detained there by sickness. Gallus eventually built himself a cell on the spot where the monastery of St. Gall now stands, and proceeded to publish the Gospel with great success in the neighbourhood of Zurich and Constance. In fortitude and devotion to his Master's service, he was inferior to none of the missionaries of those days. St. Gall, a town and canton in Switzerland, derives its political existence from this Irishman. Pepin, mayor of the palace in France, founded an abbey for this missionary, which soon became one of the principal seminaries of Europe; and from thence the seed of eternal life was scattered over a large portion of the territories of the Alemanni. The children of emperors and of neighbouring princes were many of them educated there. St. Gall, at the age of ninety-five, departed to his rest, at the dwelling of his ancient friend, Willimar, in Arbon, and was interred in his cell. Another of Columbanus's companions, named Sigebert, had also remained behind, at St. Gothard's,* near the source of the Rhine, to testify to the wild Rhetians of the salvation of Christians. He founded the celebrated Abbey of Dissentis,† in the Grisons country, from whence the light of Divine truth penetrated afterwards into the deep valleys of the Rhetian Alps.

In returning to our inquiries after the progress of Divine religion amongst the Anglo-Saxons, and of those who, in any way, contributed thereto, mention must be made respecting Aldhelm, whose education had been chiefly conducted by Adrian, the learned friend of Theodore, the Archbishop. After visiting Rome, Aldhelm was made Abbot of Malmesbury. Besides having rendered other good service to the Anglo-Saxon Christians, he supplied them with a translation of the Psalter into their own language, and did not hesitate turning his other abilities to the service of the poor: for we learn from the note-book of King Alfred, that, having observed with pain that the peasantry had become very negligent of and at their

* Columbanus is the patron saint of the parish of Hospital, at the foot of St. Gothard. See page 109.

† A very humble house of refuge and a chapel have existed for centuries at Hospice, on the top of St. Gothard, owing their origin to the Abbot of Dissentis, and where still a few monks are stationed to attend to the spiritual and temporal wants of travellers.

religious duties, he watched his opportunity, stationed himself, in the character of a minstrel, o[n a] bridge, and there he soon collected crowds of hea[rers] by the beauty of his verse. When he found that [he] had gained possession of their attention, he gradu[ally] introduced, amongst the popular poetry which he [was] reciting to them, words of a more serious nature; [and] at length he succeeded in impressing upon their mi[nds] a truer feeling of religious devotion. He was, late [in] life, advanced to the newly-founded see of Sherbor[ne] and died, after having held it four years. [A.D. 70?]

The Venerable Bede, the father of Anglo-Sa[xon] ecclesiastical history, was cotemporary with these tim[es,] being born at Jarrow, in the diocese of Durham, [A.D.] 674. Losing his parents, his relations sent him, [at] seven years of age, to the monastery of Wearmou[th,] and he appears from his youth to have been devo[ted] to God. He afterwards removed to the neighbour[ing] monastery of Yarrow, where he gave himself much [to] the study of Scripture and prayer. Writing religi[ous] and literary works, and teaching, were the const[ant] employment of his life. Knowledge of a gene[ral] character was then more familiar in the British I[sles] than in any part of Europe, and the Bishop of Ro[me] invited him warmly to the metropolis of the Chur[ch,] as Rome was then considered; but in the eyes [of] Bede, the great world had no charms. The Bish[op] of Rome dying, he was happily released from [the] invitation, and it seems that he never left his nat[ive] land. Bede appears to have been sensible, that it [is] by the grace of God that the most profitable kno[w]ledge of the Scriptures is acquired, and accordin[gly] he mixed prayers with his studies of Holy Writ.

Though genuine godliness is pourtrayed on the f[ace]

of his writings, the ignorance and prevailing opinions of the age also stand forth. They exhibit little of originality, but form, however, a copious repository of national religious tradition. In this view they are highly valuable, for they afford unquestionable evidence against Romish claims to the ancient faith of England. Nor is it amongst the least recommendations of his interesting annals, that in them also appear so many traces of Britain's more ancient Church. This Anglo-Saxon partisan of Rome likewise bears witness, that Paganized England was more than half evangelized by the holy zeal of British missionaries. His early prejudices filled him with partial gratitude to Rome; yet, as a mere historian, he weakens importantly the desires and pleadings of her advocates. Bede's last sickness continued for a fortnight, yet, during this time of suffering—from asthma, he was employed in a translation of the Gospel of St. John into the Saxon, or old English language, in which he persevered, till the youth, who had acted as his scribe on this occasion, wishing to have the work completed, reminded him that one chapter only remained to finish it; and then, that the last sentence alone was wanting. "Write quickly then," said Bede, and, giving him the closing words, he shortly after breathed his last. This event took place at his favourite abode—the monastery of Yarrow;. but each succeeding year increasing the splendour of his fame, monkish cupidity was eager to provide him with a more conspicuous tomb. His bones were accordingly transferred by stealth to Durham, and inclosed in the same coffin with the saintly Cuthbert.

[A. D. 732.] One of Bede's most illustrious friends was Elbert, who finally became Archbishop of York.

He had been the early instructor of the talented and future-celebrated Alcuin; but on his election to that see, his pupil continued under the direction of Elbert, his successor both in the seminary and see of York. When Elbert became Archbishop, he ordained Alcuin, who was a native of that place, deacon, and where he remained for a time as teacher, and in which he succeeded admirably; but his fame as a scholar resounded to Rome, whither his labours were unexpectedly transferred from the ancient city for which he had gained such celebrity. In returning from Rome, bearing the pall for his former pupil, Eanbald, who had been placed, on the death of Elbert, in the see of York, Alcuin, at Parma, first saw Charlemagne; who, being anxious to retain him, arrangements were entered into between them for the same; and accordingly, in 782, Alcuin reappeared before the Frankish conqueror. Though valued and highly favoured by Charlemagne, and usefully employed on the Continent, Alcuin pined for home, where his humble mind longed to be engaged in pious exercises and learned labours amidst scenes familiar to his youth.

[A.D. 790.] Alcuin was at length permitted to return to his native isle, to negotiate a treaty between his Royal patron and the Mercian, Offa. Having effected this, after a sojourn of three years, he recrossed the sea, to live in splendour, but in exile. Although abundant error and superstition had established themselves in the Church of Rome; and Boniface the Third had assumed the title of Universal Bishop; the introduction of idolatry under the ambiguous name of image-worship, did not appear fully developed till the time of Gregory the Second: and in consequence of his maintaining it, he has been considered and mentioned by some historians as the first Pope. To oppose this enormity in Christian Churches, which not only divided them, but kingdoms also, the brilliant talents of Alcuin were called forth by Charlemagne and his own fellow-countrymen; and in the execution of this task (known as the Caroline books) he excited the greatest admiration. In later days the Roman Catholics sought to suppress and destroy these books, but Protestants, aware of their value, concealed and preserved them.

This pre-eminent scholar was a distinguished commentator on Scripture, and he recommends, in the following manner, the study of that inestimable book: "Would we ever be with God? Let us pray and read. In the former of these exercises we converse with our heavenly Father; in the latter he converses with us. Would we sufficiently feed our souls? The Bible must supply us with the means. It is no less needful for such an end than earthly viands are for corporeal nutriment. Would we travel securely through the world? Holy writ must shed its light across our course." In ignorance of Scripture, Alcuin saw "famine and blindness weighing down the soul." In a close acquaintance with the holy book, he discerned a due supply of that celestial nutriment which ripens men for a mansion in their Almighty Father's tranquil, spotless, everlasting home. God grant that every reader of these pages may so profit by the foregoing observations, that, taking the Word of God as the only lamp to cast a light on their path through this vale of trial and temptation, each may finally rest from his labours in that blessed abode!

CHAPTER XI.

Irish Missionaries.—Ina.—Peter's Pence.—Offa.—Egbert, sole King of England.—Ethelwolf.—Alfred.—Danish Invaders subjected to Church Rates, &c.—Athelstan.—Erection of Churches.—Dunstan; Introduction of Benedictine Monks.— Ethelred.—Canute.—Elfrid.—William the Conqueror.

WE must now revert, for a short space, to the page of Ireland's history, for the purpose of noticing only one of her many distinguished missionaries, who, appearing in every part of Europe about this period, have induced Romish writers to assert, that they resorted to Rome to crave apostolic leave and license, before they preached to Pagan nations. So far from this being the case, the advocates of Roman supremacy have never yet produced a single well-authenticated case in which a Bishop of Rome sanctioned a mission, before it left the shores of Ireland.*

In the year 685, an Irish missionary, named Killian, and his companions settled in Wurzburg, where the heathen Duke of Thuringia, whose name was Gosbert, then resided. Killian preached successfully in all the provinces of the Maine, and Duke Gosbert himself was the first to receive baptism. Many of his Court, and nearly all the eastern portion of the Franks soon followed his example. It was, however, the will of God, that Killian should meet with the same fate as John the Baptist. The Duke, like Herod, had

* Dean Murray's "Ireland," page 81.

taken Geilana, his brother's wife, to be his consort: Killian prudently waited till the Duke's confidence in him was established, and he then represented to him, that his connexion was sinful, and must be dissolved. The Duke promised to comply, but postponed doing so till his return from an expedition, which he was then obliged to undertake. The danger of procrastination against the light of conscience was never more strongly illustrated; for, during his absence, the German Herodias caused the missionary, with his assistants, to be seized and beheaded in prison, in 688.* The murderers and the contrivers of the murder are said to have come to a horrible end by the righteous visitation of God, which they could not escape; and the remembrance of the venerable martyr and many of his followers was hallowed, for centuries, among the people to whom he was sent to bring the glad message of salvation. The Cathedral of Wurzburg was erected in the eighth century, on the spot where Killian, who is now considered the apostle of Franconia, suffered martyrdom. The idols which Killian had caused to be thrown into the River Maine were found, many centuries afterwards, when the foundation of a bridge over that river was being laid, and are now preserved in a house close to the Cathedral.

Willibrod, an Anglian, is the next missionary we will mention, who, with eleven others of his countrymen, went to Holland, and laboured amongst the Friezlanders; where, after suffering persecution, they propagated Divine truth with great success:

* These servants of the Most High God were immured in a close wall, in their clerical attire, with the book of the Gospel in their hands.

Willibrod being ordained Bishop of Williburg by the Roman prelate, while his associates spread the Gospel through Westphalia and the neighbouring countries.

The missionary, whose biography is more especially connected with the political history of the Anglo-Saxon Church at this period, is Winifrid, who was born at Crediton, in Devonshire; and who, emulating the pious example of his countryman, Willibrod, crossed the sea, to preach the Gospel to the Continental Pagans. He laboured with success; but eventually seems to have fallen so much under the influence of Gregory II., who consecrated him bishop under the suspicious name of Boniface, that ultimately he appears to have become bent on lowering the tone of his native country's independence, and to have engaged in an endeavour to lead it over to Papal submission. He was a personal friend, unhappily, of Cuthbert, Archbishop, and through his means endeavoured, at a Council held at Cloveshoo, in Kent, [A. D. 747] to impose on the Anglo-Saxons some favourite canons from the See of Rome. In several particulars his countrymen consented to follow Boniface; but they patriotically disregarded his example when it would have led them to compromise their dignity as a nation, by professing submission to a foreign ecclesiastical authority. Though excessively and unwisely attached to the Roman See, Boniface (Winifrid) appears to have been a man of genuine piety, as may be gathered from his letters, &c., &c., to Daniel, a conscientious prelate of Winchester, and others of his countrymen, which prove that the reformation of the clergy and conversion of the Infidels were the real objects of his zeal, and eventually he sealed a Christian profession with his blood, in company with fifty-two others, on the plain of Dockheim, where he arrived to baptize some converts, when the angry Pagans fell upon them and slew all. Other useful and pious missionaries from England and Ireland laboured on the Continent for the conversion of the heathen: but it would render the list too long to attempt to name more; and therefore we must pass on to remark, that great political changes, effected much towards the increase of the grandeur of the Papal See, which was now raised from the brink of ruin to that of a most powerful temporal sovereignty, through the interference of Pepin, King of France, in favour of Pope Stephen II.

Ina, King of Wessex, also established a scholastic foundation at Rome, to be supported by an annual tax of a penny, levied on each family in his kingdom, under the title of Peter's Pence.

It may be observed, that the political aspect of the Anglo-Saxon nations, after the Council of Cloveshoo, still further tended to effect an opening for Romish influence amongst them; for artful and ambitious men of all professions succumbed, as they ever do, to its encroachments, for the purpose of furthering their own individual and selfish purposes; and thus accelerated the spiritual and temporal bondage of their native country.

In these matters none bore a more conspicuous part than the already mentioned Offa. In his political balance he weighed archbishops and kingdoms, and then contrived that the Pope's Legates should preside at the Council of Calcuith, [A. D. 787] and thereby turn the scale in favour of Romish Canons. Offa summed up his remorseless career of sanguinary wars and treacherous political crimes by that of private murder; the victim being his intended son-in-law and guest. For this offence he journeyed to Rome for pardon, and obtained it for 365 marks. On his return home, still further to atone for his sin, he gave large landed estates to the Cathedral at Hereford; and to secure the same more effectually, he erected and endowed a splendid abbey, where it was asserted, that, by a miracle, the bones of Alban, the protomartyr of Britain, had been discovered to him and his bishops. The Pope exempted this monastery from all native authority, carefully rendering it, however, subject to that of Rome. Grateful for this favour, Offa settled a further maintenance of a Saxon penny on Ina's seminary at Rome, to be yearly levied on every family within his dominions whose lands amounted to thirty pence; and these impositions on the private means of individuals continued to be remitted till the time of the Reformation.

We may, however, now observe, that though religion had been tampered with for the purposes of ambition, and had degenerated into political craft; and, through Offa's influence and intrigues, the national dignity had been first impaired, by submitting, at the Council of Calcuith, to a Papal recognition, that power did not effect all its purposes. The Anglo-Saxons still remained firm against the introduction of image-worship; yet error upon error was gradually and imperceptibly gaining the ascendancy amongst them: the Divine life was also clogged with the asthma of superstition, and we accordingly shall henceforth find that the religion of the Gospel will gradually fade beneath our pen, and the future history of the Anglo-Saxon Church, instead of being a recital of the triumphs of Christianity, will sink into mere records of increasing superstition, spiritual declension and political handicraft, till the dark ages being fairly set in under Papal rule, tales of persecution will alone testify who belonged to the Church of Christ.

Not many years after the decease of Offa, the page of history introduces his grandson Egbert to our notice, as sole monarch of that part of Britain which had acquired the name of England. The late subdivisions of the Saxon Heptarchy were no more to be traced on her map, or her inhabitants henceforward to yield obedience to more than one sovereign; and this dignity descended to Egbert's younger son, Ethelwolf, who was summoned from a cloister and the duties of a sub-deacon in Winchester Cathedral, to the sway of this extended sceptre, at a period when energy of character as a statesman, and martial knowledge, were pre-eminently required of England's King to check the harassing invasions and plundering inroads of the Danes. The time had arrived when the retributive punishment of the Anglo-Saxons for their cruelty and injustice towards the British race was to be frightfully retaliated on their own, by successive hordes of these pirates, who, issuing from their ancestral homes, crossed the German ocean for the purposes of plunder, which, being easily obtained, and yielding them an abundant booty, subjected several generations of the English to the bitterest wrongs and sufferings. By this Danish scourge, the brilliant literary fame of the Anglo-Saxons was likewise to be swept away. Monasteries being naturally searched and pillaged for wealth, their libraries were unhappily and irretrievably despoiled and destroyed. The fatal influence, likewise, of the corrupt and degenerate religious principles which the laity had timidly permitted to be introduced into their national Church, they were also to reap the fruits of, in the enervated and faulty character of Ethelwolf, their monarch, who had been educated by St. Swithin under its special training and fostering care. Thus, instead of advancing to meet his country's foes, Ethelwolf superstitiously tried to propitiate the favour of heaven, by granting to the English Church legal security for those tithes which had *never* been withheld from it. Ethelwolf then departed for Rome, taking his youngest son, Alfred, with him. There he rebuilt the school founded by Ina, and renewed and confirmed the oppressive grant of his predecessors on his subjects for Peter's pence; and still further provided for their discontent and contempt, by not' returning amongst them as he left them—an elderly widower; but accompanied by the youthful and beautiful Judith, a princess of France, as his queen. This step involved him in private and public broils to the end of his life. Alfred, his youngest son, had twice during his childhood journeyed to Rome, and on one occasion had been crowned by the Pope; and ultimately, from untoward and unexpected events, he was called upon to take possession of the uneasy throne, for which the sovereign Pontiff, it appears, had previously destined him. In the early part of Alfred's reign he seems to have been intolerant and haughty in disposition, and to have succumbed under the accumulating difficulties of his situation; but eventually he triumphed over the Danes, and compelled them to settle in the eastern counties, and to receive baptism, stipulating also for their payment of tithes—Rome shot, light shot, and plough shot; thus compelling these new settlers to conform to the ancient rates or provisions, made by those regular payments for the exigencies of public worship, independent of tithes. What private owner of an estate can produce a title for his property so old, by many centuries, as this monarch's constitutional recognition (when he treated with his newly-adopted subjects) of the Church's title to a rent-charge upon it for the due celebration of Divine worship, &c. ?

Alfred conferred benefits of a lasting literary character on the now benighted Anglo-Saxons by his own personal exertions in translating (independent of parts of Scripture) valuable theological and historical works into their own language. These services cannot however wipe away the reproach lingering around his name, of having been an accessory in wilfully expunging the second commandment from the Decalogue, thus proving his leaning towards Romish error and innovations; and he also connived at the naturalization amongst his subjects of the decrees of the second Council of Nice, [A.D. 987], in favour of image-worship. How may we trace the gradual progress of error in nations and individuals! The leaning we thus observe in Alfred towards the See of Rome had probably been imbued during his youthful visits there, and which, accordingly, inclined him to sanction the insidious views of her ambition, to the great injury of his native country's religious belief. He resisted, however, that grand distinctive feature of modern Romanism—transubstantiation, which that Church's immediate followers were then invited to avow. John Scotus Erigena, an Irishman, who most successfully and prominently opposed this startling novelty, received Alfred's decided countenance and protection. He treated him as a friend, and placed him at Oxford, where, though really a good man, from maintaining too harsh a discipline amongst his pupils, and indulging in a severe, though jocose, style of conversation, he fell beneath the vengeance of their *penknives;* and his memory, though highly valued by sound theological writers, has received the honourable brand of heresy from Romish ones.

During these eventful times, the Irish clergy still supported their character as faithful, learned, and able opposers of Romish corruptions, even amidst the appearance of the Danes and Normans who now infested the coast of Ireland, and continued to do so till the invasion of the Norman-Angles under Henry II.; and three centuries of invasion will suffice for the corruption of the finest national population. Before this Danish invasion, the Irish Church had considerable possessions, its resources being principally derived from lands. During the incursions of these barbarians the retreats of religion were the first objects of their avarice and fury. The clergy themselves could not escape the attendant evils and decay of discipline, learning, and manners; and considerable interruption also arising in the succession to the priesthood, the temporal and spiritual condition of the Church must have been equally reduced.

In returning to our immediate consideration of English matters, we have to state that Athelstan, the grandson of Alfred, really appeared like a monarch on the throne: he crushed the Danish power in Northumbria and the eastern counties, and extended the kingdom by wresting Exeter from the Welsh; and though a reign of such military success as his exhibited must be deficient in materials for ecclesiastical history, it is clear he maintained somewhat of a religious character. Amongst other judicious constitutions, adopted probably under his sanction, is one which attests the continuance of a laudable anxiety, long prevalent, and already alluded to, for the foundation of village churches; for one of the qualifications for the dignity of Thane did not then depend on his noble origin, but was open to every one possessed of a certain property *if he had a church on his estate.*

Athelstan seems to have countenanced the monastic system, and thus prepared the way for its triumph in England under the influence of the celebrated Dunstan, who was born in the neighbourhood of Glastonbury. We have previously read of monks in Britain and Ireland, but now we are to hear of a very different race of men to those of the primitive times. No Benedictines, though they had appeared, had yet established themselves in either of these countries; but now they were to do so under the enterprising talents, ambitious views, and energy of this pretended follower of St. Peter. Those who are disposed to read an extended account of his life, of his miracles, and personal conflict with the devil, can do so in other works;* but as only regret can be experienced by dwelling on the failings

---

* Then let such readers judge for themselves, whether Dunstan, a scholar, and the head of the Anglo-Saxon Church, with the New Testament before him, in his conduct and practices came up to the apostolic model of St. Peter, his boasted predecessor in the ministry; or rather, whether the talented Macaulay, setting that acknowledged standard aside, has not shrewdly measured his character, (and that of the system of priestcraft, which ushered in the dark ages), by that of Penda, the Pagan and barbarian beneath whose sword two Christian Anglo-Saxon monarchs fell. If, again, Dunstan's doings were only weighed in the balance of the sanctuary with the Christian principles of one of the thousand working men who unhesitatingly stepped forth in this nineteenth century, at their Sovereign's bidding, from amidst Britain's counties, as competitors for a Prize Essay, would he not rather be now declared,

of those called to high offices in the Church, and as no real benefit can be reaped by a detail of the superstitious childhood and education of Dunstan in the Isle of Avalon, and of his aspiring youth, we will pass on till we find him a highly-gifted man; but so tinctured with craft and hypocrisy, that imposing on, instead of edifying, his ignorant followers,—most probably by the power of ventriloquism and the sleight-of-hand of jugglery, Athelstan, his Sovereign and patron, became so alarmed that he banished him from Court. Checked in his schemes of self-aggrandizement, Dunstan was not, however, dismayed or defeated; and on recovering from a severe illness, renounced the world as permitted and offered to us in the Gospel, to become an aspirant after it, in the order and habit of a Benedictine monk. Edmund, the successor and brother of Athelstan, built and endowed a monastery at Glastonbury, which had formerly been called Avalon, on the site of a church which had existed there for centuries; and Dunstan being appointed its first Abbot, he may safely be styled the father of English monachism.

At a legislative assembly, holden under Edmund at London, provision was again secured for the payment of tithes, church-shot, and alms fees: from such notices it is clear, that the church-rates of after-ages are not the mere creatures of some ancient unwritten prescription, but the legitimate successors of more than one formal assessment, constitutionally imposed by the national Legislature; and other historical evidences exist which prove that tithes were not regarded as the sole fund for maintaining the public worship of

"found wanting?" and the contrast between spiritual freedom with the Bible, and spiritual and mental bondage, and its concealment be more fairly exhibited?

the nation. Dunstan survived Edmund and Edred, to prove the private and public scourge of Edrey and his Queen, Elgiva, whose tragic fates and early deaths are only noticed for the purpose of explaining the events which placed the sceptre of England in the hands of Dunstan's patron, Edgar. *Subtraction* for [from] tithes and ecclesiastical dues were, under this King, made recoverable from defaulters by civil and ecclesiastical authorities conjointly; the steadily progressing increase of rural churches required such regulations, and Edgar's ecclesiastical Legislature, bearing upon the security of the churches' patrimony, is that alone which retains any appearance of utility; for, though he established forty-eight monasteries, it must unhappily be mentioned, that the larger proportion of them reared their heads amidst a considerable mass of individual suffering; for the regular clergy, under the influence of Dunstan and his Benedictine prejudices, were driven by the hand of power, (an influence which never dies), either to become monks or relinquish the houses and livings in which they were legally seated. Under pain of losing their bread, or of being branded as irreligious by the so-called apostolic successor of St. Peter, they were obliged to renounce their spiritual and natural liberty. The evils of this system were detected and resisted by the upper and well-informed classes of society; the inferior and lower ranks did not perceive its inevitable tendency; for the public mind being enslaved and bound in the chains of superstition, timidly permitted those kings and nobles who dared to resist the encroachments of priestly power to fall victims beneath the same.

Dunstan's coadjutors in these plans for gratifying private ambition, and likewise for securing priestly power more generally, were Odo and Oswald, both Archbishops, the former of whom he succeeded as Archbishop of Canterbury [A.D. 959]; and on the premature death of Edgar, finding himself pre-eminent in the kingdom, secured the succession to Edward, and then convened a legislative meeting at Calne, to inquire into the grievances of which the regular clergy complained so bitterly. As on a former occasion at Winchester (968), the whispering of some unseen agent had dismayed and overawed the assembly, so on the present one, when Boerholm, the Scottish prelate, of commanding eloquence, advocated their cause in a style likely to produce an effect in their favour to the discomfort of Dunstan and his party, suddenly the floor gave way, and most of the auditors fell into the chamber beneath. Many were killed, more maimed for life; but by a miracle, it was affirmed, the beam which supported the part whereon Dunstan stood remained firm, and his escape was interpreted into a Divine manifestation in favour of his schemes respecting monachism. The youthful Edward soon after fell by the hand of an assassin, and during a fresh and overpowering irruption of the Scandinavians, Dunstan crowned his successor, Ethelbred, at Kingston, A.D. 979.

[A.D. 980.] Dunstan, about this period, also effected the first breach in the succession of the primitive British Church, when he consecrated Gucan Bishop of Llandaff; but two years after he was summoned to render up his account to his heavenly Master [A.D. 988]: that given by monkish writers (for the purpose, it must be presumed, of misguiding the ignorant and superstitious), of his being attended at his decease by cherubim and seraphim, is impious in the extreme, and gives a melancholy picture of the already degenerate state of the Anglo-Saxon or English Church at that period.

It is not necessary here to enter on a detail of the same, for the mere purpose of exhibiting the full extent to which a deviation from the truth prevailed, or the novelties in forms of worship, with their sure attendants—ignorance and superstition, which characterized the Anglo-Saxon Church at the death of Dunstan, its Metropolitan. We would rather remind the reader, that, from the apostolic age, error, the insidious weapon of Satan against the light of the Gospel, has tried, and will continue to direct and use, its power over every Church.

The seeds of Pelagianism had been strewn in the British Church; and when Augustine brought the glad tidings of Christianity to the Anglo-Saxons, he planted amongst them a semi-Pagan, semi-Papal Church, which in later days we find was withering under the influence of ambitious and hypocritical men bearing office within its pale, who thereby effected a still further, though not complete, prostration to its evil influence. The laity being generally, as before observed, insensible to the results of their designs, did not vigorously and firmly resist them and their principles. Probably their own insensibility and supineness arose from ignorance; for, though the holy Scriptures were not entirely denied them, copies of the Bible were very scarce, and few had access to them, as they were secured in the monasteries. The priests thus held the key of knowledge, and under the sanctimonious name of tradition, interpreted, as suited their own purposes, the standard of truth; all appeal to which they reserved to themselves, and thus the intellectual, as well as spiritual, energies of Britons were paralyzed and placed in subjection at their feet, when a dreary night of mental gloom overspread their land, and prepared the way for English Popery,—a warning to every future Protestant of this land to guard, with reverential care, the jewel of the Gospel, while in their possession, in all its simplicity and purity, lest they not only lose their own souls, but entail a curse on ages yet unborn. .

Under the wretched and humiliating reign of Ethelred, it is cheering to find, from records still in existence, that one solitary ray of literary light gleamed forth from the genius of Elfric, the celebrated Saxon writer, although he appears to have shared in the prejudices against the married clergy. His homilies, written for the service of the Church, and his other writings incontrovertibly establish what Johannes Scotus Erigena had maintained for the Anglo-Saxon Church in the time of Alfred the Great: that she never had wavered in her valuable testimony against transubstantiation and implicit reliance on absolution—those two corner-stones of modern Romish belief. These writings show us, therefore, that God had not entirely forsaken this island during these disastrous times; neither could the zeal of our ancestors, as missionaries, have quite evaporated; for, through their efforts, the light of the Gospel penetrated into Norway, especially by the means of Bernard and Guthebald.

[A.D. 1001.] In the year 1001, at the desire of Olaus, King of Sweden, some English priests were sent over into the north. Of these, one was Sigefrid, Archdeacon of York. His labours were very successful, and he was made a bishop there, although his nephews were murdered by the nobility of the land. Gotebald, another English missionary, preached the Gospel with success in Norway, and was appointed a bishop in that country. There seems abundant proof that Norway, Sweden, and Denmark, were chiefly evangelized during these times by Anglo-Saxon missionaries.

[A. D. 1008.] Ethelred held a legislative assembly in 1008 at Ensham, and, amongst its ecclesiastical sanctions, is a particular statement, describing when the dues to the Church were to be paid. Soul-shot was to be paid at the opening of a grave, an obviously acknowledged authority for burial fees in those early times. During an inroad of the Danes, the unwarlike Ethelred fled into Normandy to save his life, while his subjects felt all the miseries which might be expected from victorious barbarians. While besieging Canterbury, [A.D. 1013,] the pious and exemplary Archbishop, Alphage, refusing to flee before them, was thrown down and stoned, whilst praying for his enemies and the Church, and at length a Dane, lately become a Christian, despatched him to free him from his pain.

[A. D. 1017.] The Danes got possession of the kingdom in 1017, and under the discerning eye of Canute, Ethelred's successor on the throne, the unquestionable superiority of the already mentioned Elfric so recommended him to that Danish monarch's favour, that, in spite of the obscurity in which monkish historians * have tried to involve his history, he can be satisfactorily traced to the Archbishopric of York, and he probably survived till within fifteen years of the Norman conquest.

Whilst England thus suffered from Danish invasion, so did Ireland; and equally, during the incursions there of those piratical tribes, the retreats of religion and literature became the objects of their fury. "The gentry of the old Milesian race were worn out and

* Lingard, for one.

degenerate," and their successors combined the ferocious brutality of the invaders with those more dastardly and contemptible vices which characterise a tarnished and decaying civilization. They did not allow either birthright or independence to the mass of the people, but held them in the most abject bondage of feudal servitude. The favourite exploits of these Danish invaders were the plundering and burning of churches and colleges. Of the bishops' lands, the greatest part was seized by the chieftains, and the better to secure to themselves the temporalities, they intruded even upon their spiritual functions. The princes in the territory in which Armagh was situated usurped the title as well as the demesnes of the successor of St. Patrick; and these foreigners, after their conversion to Christianity, instead of uniting with, and restoring the purity of, the ancient Church of Ireland, and reviving the splendour of those institutions and literary seminaries which their Pagan zeal had almost annihilated, introduced, in the tenth century, the Benedictine order of monks.

The brief reigns of Canute's two sons afford no materials for our subject of inquiry, nor does that of the succeeding one of Edward the Confessor. [A.D. 1042.] He founded the noble abbey of Westminster, and, among monastic writers, he has acquired much celebrity; but his Norman education made him indiscreetly partial to the French. He raised Robert, a monk of Jumieges, first to the See of London, and then to that of Canterbury, and by patronising numbers of them, gave a powerful influence to their language and manners. At length, natural antipathies and envy being effectually aroused, a powerful combination drove many of them back to the Continent; and Stitgand, Bishop of Winchester, had Canterbury bestowed on him. In this act England manifested a feeling of ecclesiastical independence, which ought not to be forgotten; nor any reader permit himself to be imposed upon by the assertions of some who falsely boast of her dependance upon Rome, in such and other matters, from Augustine to the Reformation.*

The throne of Scotland, during these disturbing days of political and religious strife, was adorned by the piety of Margaret, an English princess, who had married Malcolm, King of that country. She effected a great change not only on the ferocious spirit of her husband, but was also enabled to reform the kingdom of Scotland in a great degree, and to introduce a more serious attention to the duties of the Lord's-day, than at that time generally prevailed there. Margaret took uncommon care of the education of her children, and the fruits of her labours appeared in their lives, as three of her sons reigned successively, and were esteemed excellent monarchs. When the bitter news of her husband's death in battle was brought to her, her reflections concerning it were truly Christian: "I thank thee, O Lord, that this great affliction is sent evidently to purify me from my sins. O Lord Jesus Christ, who, by thy death, hast given life to the world, deliver me from evil." A princess of such piety, though sadly tinctured with Popish error, and bigoted to its ritual, we may hope shone not in vain in Scotland; but, probably, must have led many in that rude and ignorant age to think there was something real in godliness.

The discussions which had been carried on ever since the time of Dunstan between the regular clergy and

* Amongst other proofs, it is particularly worthy of recollection that Edgar, the obsequious tool of Dunstan, asserted expressly the Royal supremacy, by styling himself "the Vicar of Christ."

the Benedictines were not only in full force at the death of Edward the Confessor, but, unhappily, had so nurtured a predisposition amongst all classes of the community for any political change, that, when Harold, his unfortunate successor, built and endowed the noble Abbey of Waltham for a body of secular canons, facilities were afforded, if not offered, by the Benedictines to William Duke of Normandy, for that enterprising invasion of England whereby the ancient British Church, with the Anglo-Saxon Church and dynasty, were to be swept away,—Popery and the dark ages to usurp their place, and he to obtain for himself the title of William the Conqueror.

CHAPTER XII.

William the Conqueror.—Alterations in Church matters.—Romish Intrigues respecting the Irish Church.—William Rufus.—Anselm.—Contentions and Encroachments on the Liberty of both English and Irish Churches continued during the time of Henry I., when the Primitive British Church merged into the Anglo-Saxon.—Continued Resistance of the Irish Church to Romish Aggression.—Grant of Ireland by Adrian to Henry II.

[A.D. 1066.] UNDER the sway of the Norman line of kings, we shall only be able to trace the existence of the Anglo-Saxon Church, from its becoming the grand object of contention between the Crown and the Mitre. The unworthy and treacherous means resorted to by those who generally wore the latter, to resist the encroachments of the former on the property of the Church, will exhibit to the attentive and impartial reader the character and motives of both parties in their true light, and will lead him into regions of spiritual darkness; he will henceforth have to wend his way, (till the period of the Reformation), through a land of deserts and pits, a land of drought and of the shadow of death; and he will be carried by every step into scenes still more gloomy than the preceding. Here and there, indeed, a glimmering ray of the Sun of Righteousness will appear, but it will be in vain to look for any steady lustre of Evangelical truth or holiness.

From the differences which had existed between the regular clergy and the Benedictines, William had been enabled to invade England under the spurious sanction of a consecrated banner, and a Papal grant; and accordingly, that power, which had by no means been so absolute therein as in the southern countries of Europe, began to be felt more strongly, and by William's appointing foreigners to offices of importance, both in Church and State, he soon enabled it to reach the same height it had attained in France and Italy. Though the Norman tyrant found this power a convenient engine for the support of his own despotic authority, he soon proved that he considered himself the head of ecclesiastical, as well as of civil power in England, by subjecting all Church property to the same services as were demanded from other lands; yet this measure, it must be owned, had become somewhat necessary, from the immense possessions of the Church, which had hitherto hardly rendered anything towards the support of the State. As a further proof of his supremacy, William forbad Churchmen, without his leave, to quit the kingdom, or to acknowledge any Pope, or to publish letters of excommunication against persons connected with himself, or to hold councils, or make canons* without his approval.

In Saxon times, the sheriffs, or earls, had properly the government of the county, but the bishop was always associated with them in judicial matters, and they journeyed together in a circuit twice a-year. In Ecclesiastical matters the bishop sat as judge, and the sheriff assisted him by inflicting temporal punishment; and when civil offences were tried, the sheriff sat as judge, and the bishop acted as his coadjutor.

This joint jurisdiction William dissolved, by ordaining that no bishop or archdeacon should submit to the

* See Appendix, No. 4.

judgment of any secular person a cause which related to the cure of souls, but that such cases should be brought before the bishop, in places he should appoint, and be there decided according to the canons and the Ecclesiastical law. He thus effected a separation between the two executive powers, the consequence of which he most probably did not contemplate, for he thereby greatly assisted the clergy in establishing their claim to a distinct, even to a Papal, jurisdiction.

Further, he could not wait for death summoning the English prelates and clergy from their benefices, for he ejected many of them to make room for his Norman followers, the dependants and vassals of the See of Rome. Pre-eminent amongst them stands forth Lanfranc, for whose promotion to the primacy of Canterbury, he deposed Stitgand. Lanfranc was an Italian monk, and of course we find him zealously supporting the encroachments and power of Rome, and attempting to confirm the absurd doctrine of transubstantiation by his influence and authority. The sufferings of the Anglo-Saxon clergy had become such, that it is said, Aldred, Archbishop of York, died, cursing with his latest breath the monarch whom he had crowned.

While these events were progressing in England, we find those Danes who had been fortunate enough to dispossess the Irish, and establish themselves in the three maritime towns of Dublin, Waterford, and Limerick, (which afforded them easy communication with other parties of their roving countrymen,) were so exceedingly jealous of all native power, that they refused to place themselves under the jurisdiction of the Bishop of Armagh, and had also such a desire to connect themselves with their Norman friends in England, that, when converted, they (the Danes) sent their bishops to Canterbury for consecration. This measure was first adopted by Silitzic, a petty Danish king, in behalf of his countryman, Donagh, when he erected Dublin into a see. On the death of Donagh, the clergy and people of Dublin elected Patrick, and recommended him to Lanfranc, the Italian occupier of the English Primacy, for consecration, which he gladly bestowed upon him in St. Paul's Church, in London, taking advantage of the circumstance to advance the cause of Romanism in Ireland, by endeavouring to lay down, in documents still extant, a precedent for his future interference in the internal regulations of the Irish Church, which had longer resisted the encroachments of Rome than the English one. Lanfranc first flattered the petty Danish and Irish sovereigns, and though it is clear nothing could afford him satisfaction so long as the Irish hierarchy acknowledged no subjection to him; that her clergy were married; and that the rites and ceremonies of that Church were not in unison with the Church of Rome; he artfully, and that in the gentlest and most cautious terms, only touched, in those communications, on such matters as could give no great offence to the Irish clergy. Incontestably, however, have they handed down to us the proof, that both the monarchy and hierarchy of Ireland remained, at that time, complete and independent, not subject even to a legate, to the Archbishop of Canterbury, nor to the Pope.

The correspondence, however, which was carried on between the Italian Primate and the Irish clergy, as it was intended, was productive of much subtle evil to the latter, for thereby some of them became prejudiced against the old religion of the country, aud disposed towards Popish innovations. Dazzled, perhaps, by the recent success of the Normans in England, and terrified by the fate of that country, they thought it better to show some condescension, rather than provoke a doubtful contest. The attentive peruser of the foregoing pages will be ready to allow that the hostile cry which is occasionally, even in our days, raised by the Irish population against the Saxons is an unjust and ignorant one; for the first trace we observe of an impression being made on either their civil or religious liberties, was effected by Danish policy, at the period under consideration, acting under the influence of Papal power.

On the death of the Conqueror, the English throne fell to the lot of his son, William Rufus, an avaricious prince, who, for the sake of appropriating to himself the revenues of the see, on the death of Lanfranc, kept that of Canterbury vacant. This evil practice on the part of the Norman princes probably contributed, in some measure, to the establishment of Papal rule in England, for some of the clergy conscientiously, and some designedly, made it the pretext for seeking assistance and redress from its authority; and thus, eventually, the liberties of both sovereign and subjects fell beneath its power. For four years William, acting under the influence, it is supposed, of Ralph Fambard, an ecclesiastic, declared none should have the see while he lived; but a fit of illness overawed his spirit, and the voice of God, speaking to him in the still whispers of conscience, so severely reproved him for his unjust retention of it, that he named Anselm, by birth a Piedmontese, and Abbot of Bec, in Normandy, to the same. [A.D. 1093.] Contentions soon arose between the monarch and this prelate respecting ecclesiastical power, and

William's seizure and alienation of several benefices was warmly opposed by Anselm, and partially so by some other bishops; but it is to be regretted that they did not conduct their opposition on the grounds and precepts of Scripture, or even according to the precedents of the primitive Church, instead of that of the Court of Rome, for the mere purpose of increasing its power and authority, since it prevented their gaining any creditable influence over the King or people. Thus they could render so little service to the Church and country generally, that Anselm, in disgust and disguise, retired to Rome. He was one of the first men of his day, as regarded learning and religious feeling, but the habits of a cloister, and his unbounded attachment to the See of Rome, led him constantly to thwart his Sovereign, and offer him unnecessary provocation. On the other hand, although the hierarchal power was not fully established in Europe, William felt the importance of restraining that assumed by the Church of Rome. Moreover, he also detected some of the errors belonging to the Popish system, and he was not one who would submit to have his mind enthralled by the debasing superstitions whereby that Church even now seeks to enslave its votaries; and, unhappily, there was no one to lead him into the way of truth; for Anselm, his proper spiritual guide, only sought to make him obedient to the will of the Pope. Under a better guide, perhaps, William's independence of character might have proved an advantage to himself and the nation; whereas, in his endeavours to resist clerical domination, he was urged into the depths of gross Infidelity and rebellion against God.

This monarch and his subjects could not discern

between the zeal of real piety and the baseness of Romish priestcraft.*

Whilst these events were progressing in England, Ireland unhappily began to yield to the effects of Papal influence, through the medium of Gilebert, a foreigner, for whom the English Primate effected an entrance into her Church, by means of Turlogh, a Danish King of Dublin, obtaining for him the See of Limerick, and also unguardedly admitting him as legate. It soon became apparent that the *legative authority* could not have been committed to safer hands, or to one more obsequious to Anselm, with whom Gilebert had been previously acquainted at Rouen, and who immediately complimented him about his rebel conduct to his sovereign, confirming his opinion by a present of twenty-five pearls. Anselm soon began tampering with the Irish clergy more generally; and endeavoured to excite their pity for his sufferings in the cause of the Church, exhorting them in his letter "to vigilance and sincerity in *ecclesiastical discipline*," artfully adding, that if disputes about the consecration of bishops, or other causes, "cannot be canonically settled amongst themselves, to bring them before him." This assumption of a supremacy over

---

* Priestcraft is a word so often unavoidably used, and with perfect fairness, as regards the practices of Papal intrigue, that it may perhaps be desirable to guard against its being misapplied, or supposed to be necessarily connected with clerical or priestly offices. It is a term only applicable to any religious fraud, or religious influence assumed and exercised for ulterior, selfish, or political purposes, and is, therefore, an incipient evil, which, though inherent in the Romish Church, may exist and be nurtured in any other, or amongst any other denomination of religious congregations or communities of the present day.

the Irish Church, and the right of appeal, had a direct tendency to destroy its ancient independence.

Turlogh, the Irish monarch, had virtually surrendered his legal rights to the Pope, when he recommended Donogh O'Haingly to succeed Patrick in the See of Dublin. Murtogh, who mounted the throne after Turlogh, joined his nobility and clergy in a similar act of indiscretion, when they sent Malchus to be consecrated at Canterbury. Murtogh, who was involved in perpetual broils with his family and the provincial kings, hoped, by these concessions, to derive no small aid from the power and friendship of the English Primacy towards the subjugation of his own rebellious subjects. Anselm did not omit to take advantage of the opening thus offered him by the Irish monarch; for he addressed to him two epistles, in which we find him mentioning the *uncanonical* state of the Irish Church, and he specifies, in proof of his assertion, the instances notified by his predecessor, Lanfranc,* and advises him to call a council to correct these errors, and to regulate ecclesiastical affairs: and this the Irish King did in A.D. 1111, when he convened the nobility and clergy in a place called Aonguss-grove, in the plain of Magh-Breassail, in Meath, where there was a wood sacred to religion, from the remotest ages, and which, on account of ancient prepossessions, was used in order to give greater solemnity to the proceedings. The number of clergy amounted to 58 bishops, 317 priests, 60 deacons, with many of inferior orders. The same year another council was held in Meath, under the presidency of the Pope's Legate, when the numerous and petty dioceses of that district were reduced to *two*. These

* See page 138.

attempts to reduce the number of the Irish sees, and augment thereby their individual revenues, rendered the clergy more wealthy, and the Church more manageable by the Pope and his Legate. It required, however, time to accomplish such designs; but an unhappy beginning was then first accomplished in the plan adopted by Rome and England for the subjugation of the Irish Primitive Church, which proved eventually but too successful: for the decrees made at the aforementioned council were the following:—That the clergy were in future to be exempt from taxation and secular laws; and whatever they contributed to the support of the State was to be considered a free gift. The bishops were to resign their right of consecrating bishops at pleasure, and their number was to be henceforth limited to twenty-eight.

These decrees, however, can never be esteemed the avowed sentiments of the national clergy; for only about a sixth part of the Episcopal order consented to them, notwithstanding all the efforts of the monarch and his associates in favour of the Romish party. They were the production solely of those who had embraced their views, and were under the influence of the English Primate. The Irish King was actuated also by private motives, and in writing to Anselm, he thanks him for his mediation, adding, "Be assured I will obey your commands." Private purposes was the spring that set in motion his zeal, and made him perfectly obedient to Henry I., (now seated on the English throne,) and to the English Primate, who had returned from exile on the death of William Rufus. We need not doubt, therefore, that Anselm used his own and Henry's influence in urging the Irish monarch to new-model that Church, and bring it into complete subjugation to the See of Rome. In England Anselm also exercised his authority over her monarch to a great extent; for, after long-continued disputes and struggles on the subject of lay investiture,* in which the Pope took no small interest, it was yielded, that the King should no longer have anything to do with the spiritual functions of the clergy, and that they should only do homage to him as their civil ruler, for the temporal estates attached to their sees. [A.D. 1108.]

A compromise having thus been made as to both the monarchical and national privileges, Henry soon consented to advance still further the power of the Pope, by enforcing the celibacy of the clergy; but he so steadily opposed the claims of his Legate to paramount authority, that the latter took his departure and returned to Rome. Meanwhile, matters had not progressed in Ireland as smoothly as had been expected. According to the common manœuvre of designing persons of all times, the Irish clergy had been cajoled by proposals and schemes for reformation, which, being such as they could not decently oppose, they acquiesced in, to a certain extent; but when they found the unreasonable length to which affairs were likely to be carried, viz., that their ecclesiastical polity was to be dissolved, and that they and their Church were to

* The question at issue between the parties was, in fact, whether the investiture should be received from the Sovereign or the Pope; and accordingly it was agreed in those unhappy times, that the prelates should receive investiture from the Pope for spiritual jurisdiction, and at the same time do homage to the King for the temporalities of their sees.

become dependant on the nod of a Roman Pontiff, we find that the clergy and burgesses of Dublin informed Radolphus, (who succeeded Anselm in Canterbury,) that the bishops of Ireland felt the greatest indignation towards him for not accepting their ordination, and desiring them to be under his (Radolphus') spiritual dominion. But it was too late, and after some unsuccessful struggles, Malachy, a zealous champion of the new religion, ascended the Irish Archiepiscopal chair. He introduced, amidst much resistance from some parties, the order of Cistercians into Ireland, A.D. 1140; and, by the *criminal inattention* and inconsiderate sacrifices made by the petty princes of Ireland, and by the unabating zeal of its designing supporters, Romanism daily gained ground in that country. Henry I. having reduced Wales into an English province, invaded its religious liberty, and soon endeavoured to destroy the distinctive character of the British Church, which had there successfully resisted, for above eleven centuries, all endeavours to shake her independence. This he attempted to effect through the appointment of Bernard, a Norman, as suffragan bishop of St. David, by making him, at his consecration, profess subjection to the See of Canterbury. The plot, when probably no native would be found to yield himself a mere clerical tool for the spiritual and temporal enslavement of his countrymen to Papal power, did not, however, then entirely succeed; for Bernard, soon after his appointment, refused to act upon this profession, and the independence of the See of St. David's remained during that and the two succeeding reigns. The Papal power and interests were the only ones advanced by the miseries which prevailed in England and Ireland during the reign of Stephen, who was deprived of his patronage, as well as of the fidelity, of his subjects, from the facility with which oaths and declarations were made and broken, and perjury sanctioned by Rome and such of her emissaries as resided amongst them. The clergy were also subjected to a foreign legate; abbeys were freed from *episcopal* jurisdiction, holding directly from the See of Rome, and forming ecclesiastical garrisons prepared for its defence.

[A.D. 1155.] Stephen's successor, Henry II., contributed much to the augmentation of the Roman power, and extended its jurisdiction throughout the world, when he accepted the grant of Ireland from Pope Adrian, in a bull, which gave him permission to enter the said Ireland "for the extension of the borders of the Church," (Papal,) and the collection of Peter's pence. In the perusal of the bull* itself, nothing can be more clear than the inference, that at the date of Adrian's bull, Ireland was not considered within the boundaries of the Romish Church; for else how could those boundaries be extended by Henry's invasion? It is also evident therefrom, that the Irish had never been in the habit of paying Peter's pence, and that both in doctrine and discipline they differed widely from the Romish model. This conveyance and the subsequent negotiations between Henry II. and the Pope were secretly conducted, until circumstances had effected a lodgment for English arms in Ireland. A confirmatory letter, however, appeared in a few years, which was read in a Synod at Cashel, and the two edicts were

* See Dean Murray's "Ireland," page 105.

solemnly promulgated by a Synod held at Waterford, when Henry was formally proclaimed "Lord of Ireland," and the severest censures of the Church (Papal) were denounced against all who should impeach the donation of the Holy See, or oppose the government of its illustrious representative.

Previous to this period, it is demonstrated by historical facts, that—1st. The Irish ecclesiastics had never taken oaths to the Pope.

2d. They never applied to the See of Rome for bulls of nomination, institution, or exemption.

3d. They never appealed to Rome for the decision of ecclesiastical causes.

4th. The bishops and prelates of a tribe were appointed by the chieftain, either directly, or with the previous form of an election by the priesthood.

5th. Papal legates had no jurisdiction in Ireland until the twelfth century, and then their jurisdiction was limited to the English settlements.

The splendid bribe of full one-tenth of the produce of all other lands, and more than a third of all moveable property, and protection from injury extending over its own possessions, was bestowed on what may be designated the Anglo-Irish Church, at these councils. For, on the testimony of Dr. Lunigan, we find that wherever the *natives* maintained their *independence,* "*clergy and people followed their own ecclesiastical rules, as if the Synod of Cashel had never been held.*" Such was the origin of "the two Churches in Ireland: the one, the *Primitive Episcopal Church,* of the real native Irish clergy and people; the other, that of the Anglo-Norman Popish aristocracy, which, though of foreign growth, had certain facilities for striking root, and overwhelming any rival one by the weight of its branches, which the principles of vital Christianity did not allow to its pristine opponent. Yet, notwithstanding every disadvantage, the native Church continued to exist for three centuries; and even discovered some signs of life as late as the reign of Henry VII.

This is bad, because it shows that the present Irish Church is from Rome & not from St. Patrick & are rebels to their not

The Pope has no ... power in Austin ... my church was founded

CHAPTER XIII.

Henry II. invades and proclaims himself King of Ireland.—Heretics first condemned as such at Oxford.—Thomas-à-Becket.—Crusades.—John.—State of Church in Ireland.—Robert Grossetête, Bishop of Lincoln.—Dominicans and Franciscans introduced into England.—Henry III.—Remarks on Ireland.

ALTHOUGH Pope Adrian's grant of Ireland to Henry II. had been made in the second year of his reign, he personally remained long inactive; but the friendly intercourse which, from time immemorial, had existed between the inhabitants of the opposite shores of Cardiganshire and Ireland was now to be interrupted; and the first hostile foe from Wales pressed the soil of Ireland when Fitz-Stephen, a Welsh knight, under the pretext of assisting Dermod, King of Leinster, in a private quarrel, invaded the country; and, being successful, and reinforced by Strongbow,[*] aspired to the sovereignty; which rousing and alarming Henry, he forbad assistance to be rendered him, and soon appearing himself at the head of an Anglo-Norman army, announced himself as King of Ireland; and, as a proof of the same being no empty title, made a present

[*] In effecting an entrance into Ireland, Strongbow hesitated on which side he should disembark to march to Waterford. On inquiring the names of two places which he saw, he was informed one was the tower of Hook, and the other the church of Crook. "Then," said he, "shall we advance and take the town by Hook or by Crook," and hence originated one of our national proverbs.

of the city of Dublin to his good citizens of Bristol.
[A.D. 1172.]

The Irish chieftains, though compelled to show some exterior signs of submission to Henry, never thought of renouncing their own authority, or the customs of their forefathers, and were therefore driven into the worst parts of the country by their conquerors, who hoped to extirpate them by an incessant warfare. But this was far from being the case; and, from their strong attachment to the religion of their ancestors, and the native priests also continuing to follow their own rules, and holding no intercourse with the bishops who were imposed upon them by English and Romish influence, they were soon stigmatized as "heretics," and the Anglo-Norman adventurers were styled "liege men," or good subjects. The Irish, unhappily, stipulated with Henry for the use of their own laws, and were thus left at the mercy of the aristocratical families, amongst whom the country had been divided, and were regarded, when they came into courts of justice seeking redress from their oppression, as aliens at the best—more frequently as enemies and rebels.

[A.D. 1179.] Scarcely had Henry returned to his hereditary dominions, than the bishops, who had rendered him assistance, presuming on the same, began to embarrass the government which he had set up amongst the *new settlers*.

In these political affrays, none bore a more conspicuous part than Lawrence O'Toole, Archbishop of Dublin, who, after an ostentatious display, for some years, of attachment to the English monarch, appeared as his accuser, taking advantage of Pope Adrian's bull for extending "the borders of the Church." As it was intended to act as a license for obtaining more temporal benefits for the clergy, he exerted himself for the privileges of the Church against the King. Henry acted prudently and wisely, and, though the Archbishop was backed by Papal power, contrived that he should pass the remainder of his life an exile in Normandy.

This manifold traitor to his Church, his native country, and his King—the sovereign, also, of his own election in his adopted country—was in due time canonized, and his protection is still invoked by the Romish hierarchy of the present day, with a publicity which displays the unshaken constancy of the order.

The English monarch, who accepted a grant from the Pope to annex Ireland to his dominions, degraded himself, in company with the King of France, by holding the bridle of the horse of Pope Alexander VII., one on each side, conducting him to his place of abode at Rheims; but the princes of the earth, as well as the meanest persons, were then bondsmen, and enslaved to the Popedom; and there seemed no end of the deceits whereby the prince of darkness was enabled to impose on mankind.

As we return to gather up the leading events which meanwhile had taken place in the Church of England, we find she had also rapidly sunk into a state of subjection to the Papal See; for although men of real sense like Henry II. *felt the temporal force of ecclesiastical oppression,* lamented, struggled, and resisted, little effect was produced. They were themselves so perfectly ignorant on spiritual matters, that they aided the Court of Rome in their persecutions of real Christians, when thirty Germans of that character sought refuge therefrom in England.* What religious and

* A remnant of the persecuted monks of Orleans.

moral darkness must then have pervaded the island, when a wise king, the renowned University of Oxford, and the whole body of clergy and laity then assembled, could unite together, and consent to persecute, even unto death, persons who for the first time were brought before them on a charge of heresy! [A.D. 1159.] Like the Gadarenes of old, it was beseeching Jesus to "depart out of their coasts."

The legendary, and partly authentic, history of Thomas-à-Becket, the first Englishman who had filled the chair of Canterbury, (since the time when Stigand had been deposed by William the Conqueror to make way for Lanfranc,) is so fully detailed in general historical pages, that it shall only be very briefly dwelt on in these. But it is perhaps desirable to point out, that the existing cause of Becket's contentions with Henry II. arose from that Primate's hypocritical reception of what are known, in Ecclesiastical history, as the Constitutions of Clarendon.* They were sixteen in number, and were framed for the purpose of affording both sovereign and people some protection from Ecclesiastical power. Becket *swore* to them, but soon obtained a *dispensation* from his *oath of the Pope*. He then fled the country for a time, but ultimately, under an assumed reconciliation with his sovereign, returned, to fall shortly afterwards by the hand of assassins, and his tomb to become the scene of Henry's superstitious and ignominious humiliation, and enrich the coffers of the monastery which contained it, by bringing pilgrims and offerings to his shrine. Becket was speedily canonized,—but wherefore?—for although he fell by the murderous hand of violence, he was no martyr. He fell as the victim of his own unchristian and unjust

* See "Short's History of the Church of England," p. 56.

efforts to rivet the supremacy of the Pope and the domination of the hierarchy on the consciences and possessions of his countrymen, and not for the faith as it is in Jesus.

From the strongly-contrasted and opposite lights and shades in which the period we have now reached (when tidings arrived from the East, that the crescent gleamed in triumph over the cross,) have been treated by different authors, as each has individually yielded to the bias of his respective religious principles or feelings; no portion of our national history has given more embarrassment to general and superficial readers: yet, amidst the conflicting testimonies of different historians we may observe that the crusades, or military expeditions of the European powers for freeing the Holy Land from the dominion of the Turks, (and to which Henry II. largely contributed in money, and for which Richard I. left his kingdom, and during whose absence his subjects suffered much from internal warfare, and from the rapacious rule of the Bishop of Ely, whom he left Regent [A.D. 1199],) were, under the overruling providence of the Most High, made of much general advantage to Christendom.

At the commencement of the thirteenth century, it seems generally allowed that the Papal power rose to its greatest height in this kingdom; probably because it found her under the rule of John, a weak, cruel, and wicked monarch. The first act of further open encroachment was exhibited in the pre-appointment of Stephen Langton to the See of Canterbury; for whenever a vacancy occurred there, it offered the Pope a crumb for the nourishment of his temporal and spiritual pride; and he applied to his designs Matthew xviii. 17, 18; and, accordingly, he annulled the choice of the sovereign and monks of Canterbury in favour of Stephen Langton, who, though an Englishman by birth, had been educated abroad, and had already been raised to the dignity of cardinal. The intemperate warmth of the English monarch was met by the haughty firmness of Innocent III., who first laid the kingdom under an interdict, and then excommunicated John.

An interdict was a severe ecclesiastical censure, by virtue of which churches were everywhere closed; all religious services were suspended, except the rite of baptism; the dead were buried in common ground, and the images and pictures of saints were taken down. Though the religious observances thus suspended were, in most respects, only unmeaning ceremonies and idolatries, we cannot but mark the atrocious conduct of this pretended minister of God, who punished the people for the fault of their King. Innocent was evidently guided by that spirit concerning which the apostle said, "Many are the enemies of the cross of Christ, whose end is destruction, whose glory is in their shame, who mind earthly things." This spirit began to exist even in the apostles' time; and it was now more openly displayed in Innocent's not hesitating to claim the power of Deity, and to apply its influence to support wicked and unchristian proceedings for the sake of filthy lucre. The subject is brought clearly to view in all its strength when we remember, that the Papacy held out that the services and ceremonials thus forbidden were not only means of grace, but the necessary passports for admission to, and for happiness in, the world to come. So that, merely for a dispute with a king respecting the appointment of an archbishop, the Pope exposed all that monarch's subjects to those sufferings which the ecclesiastics of Rome *taught* would be felt even after death. The Lord, however, manifested how insignificant the wrath of man is, when *unaccompanied* by his permission; for so little real effect had these spiritual denunciations, that the only two successful expeditions John made against Ireland and Scotland took place during this very period.

[A. D. 1212.] The Pope proceeded to depose John, and to free his subjects from their oaths of allegiance. He committed the execution of this act, the following year, [A. D. 1213,] to Philip of France. The secret cabals of the discontented barons, whose defection rendered all John's projects of defence uncertain, coupled with the threat of a foreign invasion, forced the pusillanimous monarch to surrender his kingdom to Pandulf, the Pope's Legate: and on May 15, at Dover, Pandulf restored the crown which had been laid at his feet. A tribute of 1000 marks was imposed, and the Legate, having obtained the object of the Popish Church, forbad Philip to proceed with the invasion. This latter loudly complained at being thus kept back from an enterprise undertaken at the command of the Pope for the remission of his sins. Such was the blasphemous pretension of the Papal power! So much did the Pope now consider England as his own, that when the barons, who styled themselves on that occasion "The army of God and the holy Church," compelled John to sign the grant of privileges called "Magna Charta," [A. D. 1215,] the Pope espoused the cause of John with such earnestness, that he suspended Langton, his own chosen Archbishop, for the part he had taken in the cause of liberty. John subsequently obtained a letter annulling Magna Charta from the Pope, who declared at the same time, with a profane oath, that the barons, having been instigated by Satan, should be punished,—adding a curse on both the King and barons, if they observed the conditions of the Charter. This was going too far, even for these times of ignorance. Langton, though appointed Archbishop by the Pope, conscientiously encouraged the barons and clergy to resist Papal encroachments, which, at last, became so intolerable, that the barons declared they would not admit any right on the part of the Pope to interfere in secular concerns, as our Lord only gave authority to Peter and his successors in ecclesiastical matters. Even this was allowing too much; but the world could not then understand that the ministers of Christ, whether truly such, or only so called from outward profession, have no authority to rule the consciences of men, or to "lord it over God's heritage." Let us, therefore, here pause to meditate on, and admire the wondrous ways and leadings of the Most High. The encroachments of the Pope on both the spiritual and political liberties of England led first to the abolition of regal tyranny therein, and, secondly, so materially undermined the Papal power, that from this period, it may be observed, it gradually declined in England from its meridian height, till it set in ignominy and impotence beneath the bright light of the Reformation.

While England had been placed under an interdict for her monarch's lack of obedience to the Pope, the same ecclesiastical scourge was shaken over the inhabitants of Dublin and its neighbourhood by Comyn, the successor of Lawrence O'Toole in that see, in consequence of counter-claims having been also made respecting the temporalities of it by the original proprietors of the lands, and by the Lord-Deputy, (as representative of the English monarch,) both of whom opposed those of Comyn. Being thus excluded from possession, the Romish Primate excommunicated De Valois, and all the other members of the administration; and, like his master, not content with this vengeance being laid on the transgressors, he placed the unoffending inhabitants of the city and diocese under an interdict. In the end the Lord-Deputy had to yield, and, as an atonement for his fancied misconduct, paid a handsome fine in land to the See of Dublin.

[A. D. 1210.] While the Romish party kept firm possession of the maritime and best portions of Ireland, and were also holding the throne itself in vassalage, the most scandalous enormities disgraced their clergy and prelates. The Bishops of Waterford and Lismore had a dispute concerning certain lands, and the affair was referred to Commissioners appointed, not by Government, *but by the Pope.* The secret spring of all Ireland's woe originated in the weakness of the Norman kings, after Henry had accepted the grant of that country. The *Romish* Church was the *badge of conquest*, the *badge of slavery* to *Ireland;* for its faith and power were forced upon the inhabitants at the point of Norman lances; and her sovereigns and leaders, not being able to govern or protect her, she fell a victim to the designs of the Romish party in Church and State: but a small part only of the country was occupied by English troops, and the King was the nominal "*Lord* of the Isle," while the Pope was, *ipso facto,* the sovereign of the country: and just in proportion as this policy was pursued, and which originated in the weakness of England, turbulence and dissatisfaction followed, as a matter of course, in its train.

[A. D. 1215.] About this time the Papal See, by the

Council of St. John Lateran, authoritatively declared transubstantiation to be a tenet of the Church; and, under the pontificate of Innocent III., the Inquisition was also established.

[A.D. 1216.] Though the Papal tyranny reached its ascendancy in England when it compelled John to place his crown at the feet of the Pope's Legate, its exactions and practical effects were by no means diminished under the weak reign of Henry III. A vast number of the benefices were filled by Italians, who resided out of the kingdom, and who placed therein low characters, destitute of morals, to scrape together whatever was useful and valuable, and thus enable them to live luxuriously, while the natives of the country were impoverished.

[A.D. 1235.] The English barons made a remonstrance to the Council of Lyons only to feel the inadequacy of the attempt. It was not, however, from the barons alone that the opposition to the Court of Rome now arose; for Robert Grossetête, Bishop of Lincoln, ventured to lift up his feeble voice against corruptions, which he designated "as Antichristian." Innocent IV. had named his nephew, then a child, to a canonry in the Cathedral of Lincoln; but the remonstrances of the bishop were so strong, that, although they drew from the Pope a torrent of abuse, he wisely gave way to the more prudent advice of some of his cardinals. Though the bishop's views, as far as can be judged of from his writings, may, on many subjects, be considered very indistinct, it must be acknowledged that he was a most remarkable and worthy character, fitted for the period when he appeared: and that, for a long time previous, so consistent, steady, and spiritually-minded a prelate had not been seen in England. We may therefore hope that, sheltered by obscurity, but influenced by the same Holy Spirit, Christ preserved to himself, even in these dark ages, a godly seed in England. But while one rejoices in this, we find the country, in the early part of the century, had been intruded on by the presence of two distinct orders of friars. The Dominicans, who were the founders of the Inquisition, came to England about the year 1221, and first appeared at Oxford. The Franciscans first settled at Canterbury in 1234. Both orders were the confidential agents of the Pope; and by his authority, through the means of auricular confession and other superstitious usages of the time, succeeded in very much alienating the people from the regular clergy: and, under various pretexts, exacted large sums of money from them, and fleeced even the abbots of the monasteries. The Franciscans particularly undermined their influence by pretending poverty, by begging for support, and by their public preaching.

Amongst the regular clergy, Sebal, Archbishop of York, furnishes us with an example worthy of being recorded. He wrote to Pope Alexander IV., remonstrating against his violent and oppressive conduct, and exhorted him to follow Peter—to feed, not to devour, the sheep of Christ. His courage and integrity enraged the Pope, who excommunicated him. The Romanists in England also persecuted him; but he kept possession of his see till he died.

[A.D. 1268.] The differing and conflicting interests which, however, distracted England during the reign of Henry III., led to the establishment of an assembly, drawn from the counties and boroughs, which being considered the origin of the present House of Commons, proved an event of the greatest importance in the annals of the nation. While these secular events were passing in England, the Archbishop of Dublin, having been appointed Lord Justice, and also Legate of the Holy See in Ireland, employed all the power these triple offices gave him in extending the jurisdiction of the spiritual courts. The citizens, oppressed by these new tribunals, appealed to the King, Henry III., who wrote a sharp but ineffectual letter to his deputy. The civil sword was then transferred to the hands of a layman, but the Romish clergy persevered in their career of usurpation; and after eleven years of silent endurance, the monarch was compelled to issue a writ, which still exists as a striking example and proof of the ascendancy they had attained.

[A. D. 1266.] Towards the close of Henry's long reign, Prince Edward, the heir-apparent to the throne, who had been created "Lord of Ireland," had the courage to confront the true authors of the evil. Though his spirited reprimand has been handed down to us, history has not informed us what effect it actually produced. In the Irish capital, where the image of royalty might inspire a little respect, and where the citizens had obtained a charter of special privileges, it might have effected some good; but the rest of the island apparently yielded to the misrule of the Romish hierarchy.

CHAPTER XIV.

Edward I.—Ireland.—Edward II.—The distinctive Marks of two Irish Churches at that time.—Edward III.—Bradwardine.—Edward's Efforts to retard the Encroachments of the Popish Clergy.—Partially successful in England.—Nullified in Ireland through their intrigues procuring the enactment of the Statutes of Kilkenny.

[A.D. 1272.] DURING the reign of Edward I., one of the wisest and most vigorous of our kings, it might, perhaps, be expected that we should find some relief was obtained by those of his subjects who groaned under Romish oppression; but, unhappily, the weaknesses and vices of former Norman kings, and the pusillanimity of his father, Henry, during a very long reign, had enabled the Popes to enslave the nation completely; and Edward, though very great in the political acts of peace and war, possessed no real piety; and, therefore, in ecclesiastical matters, did little for his country. Yet he paid the tribute, which the Pope had imposed on the nation during the reign of John, reluctantly, not allowing it to be called a tribute; and he constantly maintained that he was not a vassal of the Roman See. The general proceedings of Edward, and his repeated acts of opposition to the Papal power, were, however, the first of a series of political measures, which being attended by increasing light beaming on men's minds, at length delivered England from the tyranny thereof. A limit was first wisely put on the increasing possessions of the monks, who, it was found, would otherwise, in the course of a few years, have become the only landed proprietors in the country. [A.D. 1279.] This was effected by the Statute of Mortmain, a most valuable law, which forbad the holding of lands by persons who could perform no military service to the Crown and public. The doctrinal opinions of the ecclesiastics, against whose encroachments these laws had to be framed, were no less objectionable than their political or private characters. The prelates were warriors: oftener found in the field of battle than preaching; in times of peace they dwelt in military castles, and the different orders of friars pried into every rich and poor man's home; and under the guise of confessing, they beguiled the ignorant multitude into the hope of purchasing the absolution of their sins from the chief minister of the Church, who claimed to himself the power of loosing and binding. Idolatry had become excessive, through the specious intercessory worship of the Virgin Mary and the saints; and the people neglected the weightier matters of the law, placing their hopes on pilgrimages, &c., &c.

The doctrine of transubstantiation must not be omitted; for it had now gained considerable attention and credence in England, and, subsequently, formed no ordinary subject of national persecution. It was asserted, that, under the form of bread and wine, the very body of Christ was presented, which had been born of Mary and had suffered on the cross; and that the elements, after consecration, no longer retained their material substance: whilst it was added, that he who would not believe this, would have disbelieved Christ to be the Son of God, had he seen him in the form of a crucified servant.

About this period a celebrated tract appeared,

entitled, "The Ploughman's Complaint." The author is not known; but, with much energy and zeal, he described the gross and reigning abuses of the day, and it probably had some effect.

We have previously remarked how unwisely the native Irish had acted, when their country was seized on (through the Pope's grant) by Henry II., in requesting to remain under their own primitive laws. Their descendants, lingering within the precincts of the English colonies, or pent up in their old possessions, finding their situation, in consequence, most forlorn; and that all hope of expelling the strangers from their land had vanished, made up a purse of 8,000 marks from amongst a few broken clans and various smaller groups of miserable natives, which they tendered to the King, Edward I., through his Irish Governor, with a request that he would receive them as his faithful liege men, and take them under the protection of the laws of England. Nothing can so well illustrate their broken-hearted wretchedness as this mode of preferring their petition. A measure so wise, so just in itself, so fair in its prospects, so full of glory to the prince, could not even be tendered by the projectors of it,—the suppliants for it, unless, like too many of their unhappy posterity, they approached the seat of government with a bribe. This petition was preferred to the barons and prelates of Ireland, and was evaded on the ground of so many of the former being unavoidably absent. A second was then sent, which the monarch, notwithstanding the absence of the majority of the nobles, desired might be taken into immediate consideration. Thus, the ecclesiastical members, bishops, abbots, and priors, commanded a very decisive majority—in fact, the *spiritual Lords outnumbered the whole body* of lay

Peers at any time. Ireland was, therefore, once more at the mercy of the Popish clergy. These might now, by a vote, have almost atoned for the original baseness of their predecessors, and arrested the bloody progress of centuries of desolation.

[A. D. 1280.] But the law of England, even at that date, was too favourable to liberty not to be viewed with alarm by Popish men, who aimed at despotic power. It cannot, however, be ascertained from authentic records if the council above alluded to ever met. One thing only is certain, that the Popish bishops defeated the good intentions of the King, and closed their ears to the groans of the native inhabitants. This was one of the early instances of error committed, or rather permitted, by the English Government respecting the polity of Ireland; and it deserves to be added, that about fifty years after, these Irish outcasts petitioned again for naturalization on their native soil, and that their petition was again evaded by nearly the same Papal device.

[A. D. 1313.] Though on the Continent monarchs seemed to be arousing to a sense of the encroachments of the Popedom under Edward II., the weak son and successor of Edward I., it will not be supposed that England was in a condition to oppose or restrain them; and accordingly we find, that, while Ireland was being depopulated and oppressed by every species of outrage, the Parliaments were thought to be worthily employed in a ridiculous contest for precedence between the prelates of Armagh and Dublin, and in deliberating whether, in token of the same, a bishop should have his crosier borne erect or depressed. The point really at issue was, who should be head of the Church in Ireland; and in this question was involved the contest continually carried on, during the period of the ascendancy of Romanism in Ireland, between the ancient Irish and the modern Anglo-Popish Church. The Archbishop of Armagh was the Primate of the primitive Church; the Archbishop of Dublin that of the Romish Church, introduced after the invasion of the Danes.

The question was agitated for twenty years, and was then settled in the following way:—The Archbishop of Dublin was still to retain the title of "Primate of Ireland," the Archbishop of Armagh that of "Primate of *all* Ireland;" thereby carrying down to our own day the impress of its extension, its antiquity, and Protestantism.

Under the invasion and partial success of Edward Bruce, those evils, which the prelates of the last reign would *not* allow their monarch to remedy, were now converted into arguments against the government of his successor; and priestcraft shewed the versatility of its genius by reassuming the mask of patriotism. The Romish Bishops denounced the English as enemies of the Church and oppressors of the nation. They exhorted the populace to flock to the banner of Bruce, a prince, they said, of the ancient line of Milesian monarchs, and the chosen instrument of the common deliverance; and they formally crowned the adventurer King of Ireland. When the rebel priesthood had taken this irrevocable step, the experience of our own times may prepare us for finding these early ecclesiastics cautiously putting forward laymen as the ostensible agitators: and while they touched with their hands the latent springs of sedition, they slid aside from responsibility, and relinquished to their lay confederates all the really conspicuous and dangerous posts of honour. Accordingly we find that in the hope of arresting the approaching storm of Papal and Royal vengeance, they despatched to Rome a memorial, entitled, "The Complaint of the Nobles of Ireland," addressed to Pope John XXII. This extraordinary document begins with political grievances, and then proceeds to the wrongs of the Church; yet, in the concluding sentence, it tries to exculpate the prelates from any participation in the rebellion, or in the remonstrance: but the voice of history proclaims the falsehood of the denial, and the entire structure of the complaint exposes its inconsistency.

Bruce's career having terminated at the decisive battle of Dundalk, the Pontiff issued an edict,—whether, as supreme Lord of Ireland, or in his *spiritual* capacity, as head of the Church, it is not easy to determine,—granting to Edward II. a subsidy of a tenth of the revenues of his Anglo-Irish subjects for two years. The laity quietly submitted, but the clergy proved refractory, and eluded the tax. Such was the real bearing of men who had so recently represented themselves as such spirit-broken priests, that they dared not lift a voice against the oppressor of their order! Meanwhile they practised cruelties of no ordinary character on females and individuals of rank, on the plea of witchcraft, from which the English Deputy himself did not escape. The infallible Church of Rome,* during this period, began, however, to be shaken from within her own bosom. On the death of

* Roman Catholics are divided on this point. Some consider the Pope as infallible; others, that only the decrees of a general council are to be accounted so; while a third party assert, that those decrees are only to be received as infallible when confirmed by the Pope. In either of these cases the opinions of men are to be considered as the rule of faith. Such is the consequence of departing from the Word of God; and so much for the boasted *unity* of the Church of Rome.

Boniface VIII., who, by following the steps of Hildebrand, (Gregory VII.,) had filled the Christian Church with the noise and turbulence of his ambition and despotism in civil and ecclesiastical matters, the schism which then took place was a providential blessing to mankind; for, during the next fifty years, this *united* Papal Church had two or three heads at the same time; and while each of the contending Popes was anathematizing his competitor, the reverence of mankind for the Popedom itself was insensibly diminishing; and the labours of those few whom God raised up to propagate Divine truth, began to be more seriously regarded by men of conscience and probity, who, in their turn, attempted to stem the current of ecclesiastical corruption and oppression. We, therefore, find, that when Edward III. ascended the throne of England, something was done, throughout the extent of the realm, to restrain the growing power of the Popedom and her clergy.

[A.D. 1343.] By the Statute of Provisors, the rights of patrons and electors of livings were secured against the claims of the Papal See to appoint, not only to existing, but sometimes to future vacancies in the Church. As the law, however, practically carried all questions dependent on it to the See of Rome, to which the party aggrieved would naturally apply for redress, it was then enacted, that whoever drew out of the country a plea which belonged to the *Sovereign's Court* should be outlawed. Of the wisdom, justice, and necessity of these laws, as well as of the previous one of mortmain, there can be no doubt. Edward III. attempted also many salutary alterations in the polity of Ireland; but the Popish lords, abbots, and others proved too much for him. The Irish Archbishop excommunicated his Commissioner of revenue when he attempted to levy a subsidy granted by Parliament, extending the same punishment to the descendants of the third generation of those clergy who yielded to it, and the timidity of Government suffered the dispute to die away. Thus the Popish Church triumphed, by its spiritual tyranny, over the enactments of the civil powers, and thus one of the greatest of the English monarchs, a conqueror, who had routed the warlike clans of Scotland, and dispersed the chivalry and fleets of France, was "crossed and bearded" without resistance or redress, by the Romish ecclesiastics of Ireland.

Amidst the general dearth of faithful and intelligent men which also prevailed among the clergy of England, one very learned and pious man seems to have attended Edward III. in his wars in France, as his confessor. Thomas Bradwardine is the extraordinary individual alluded to. Some writers of the time ascribed Edward's signal victories and great success in arms, rather to the virtues and holy character of his chaplain, Bradwardine, than to the bravery or prudence of the kingly warrior himself. With meekness, and persuasive discretion, Bradwardine appears, not only to have often calmed his Royal master's fiery temper and warlike rage, but frequently to have addressed the army with the same desirable influence. On a vacancy occurring in the See of Canterbury, the monks elected Bradwardine to fill it; but Edward would not part with him. On another similar occasion he was again chosen by them, and Edward then, acceding to their wishes, he was consecrated at Avignon [A.D. 1349]; but not many weeks afterwards, and only seven days after his arrival in England, he died at Lambeth. His departure out of this life seems to have been a providential mercy to himself. Pious, and simple in his habits and manners, he was little fitted to have rendered much service to the Church in those trying times. His esteemed writings still exist, and though, it seems, they are more adapted for the scholar than for the mass of the people, yet they then proved powerful instruments amongst the former for general good. Bradwardine has, therefore, been styled the "Morning Star" of the Reformation, of which we shall soon perceive the dawn.

Another distinguished character also appeared in Richard Fitz-ralf. He was educated at Oxford, and promoted by Edward III. to the Archbishopric of Armagh, in Ireland. He vigorously opposed the mendicant friars, who, being greatly enraged, cited him to appear before the Pope, and give an account of the doctrine which he had broached and maintained in the pulpit and in conversation. The Archbishop, in the presence of the Pope, defended at large the rights of parochial ministers against the friars, and exposed the enormities of the latter. For this he was excommunicated, and suffered great persecution from both civil and ecclesiastical powers, and at the end of seven or eight years died in banishment. This holy man defended his tenets by his writings and works, which testify that God was with him. In general, however, the great defect of those who withstood the reigning corruptions of these times was this,—they distinctly complained of the prevailing abominations, but were very scanty in describing the real evangelical doctrines which alone can relieve and sanctify the souls of men. This remark is but too applicable to the very best of the Reformers, who appeared in Europe from this time to the era of the Reformation. That was a work

I

which well deserved its name, because it builded up as well as pulled down, and presented the Church with a new fabric as well as demolished the old. It was a work wherein the character of a Divine influence appeared far more completely than in any former attempts against Popery, and therefore its effects are lasting—they remain to this day.

Other circumstances of a general character tended to prepare the way for it during Edward III.'s reign, independent of those disputes about the Popedom, testifying to the fallibility of that power, and which have already been alluded to. We will, therefore, now remark, that, whereas the French language had been arbitrarily forced on the nation when the Norman line ascended the throne, now that of the country was permitted; and it began to be cultivated by those who formerly had restricted and neglected it. Further, those who really desired the spiritual welfare of the people dispersed vast numbers of small written treatises and translations of portions of the Scriptures in English; and, not only the middle, but the lower orders of the people, began to take an interest in their religious liberties. The good seed was thus beginning to be widely scattered throughout the land; and though it lingered two hundred years in attaining its maturity, and had to be watered with the blood of the martyrs, it eventually produced abundant fruit.

Besides the foregoing advantages, the representatives of the Commons were allowed, in this reign, to form a distinct legislative body; the knights of the shires were separated from the barons, and sat with the burgesses, which gave additional force to the Lower House of Parliament: they also chose their own Speaker, who not only presided over their deliberations, but pleaded their rights and privileges, and remonstrated against official misconduct.

[A.D. 1367.] We must now turn for a while to Ireland, whither Lionel, Duke of Clarence, second son of Edward III., went twice, to recover the vast possessions he was entitled to in right of his wife, heiress of the De Burgh family, one of the most potent of those descended from the Anglo-Norman invaders. As has been already cursorily noticed, the ancient race might have been compensated and sheltered from much actual suffering, had they been admitted to the superior comforts and privileges of Englishmen; especially, when they besought them at the footstool of Edward I., the sovereign whom they gladly acknowledged. The same object might, perhaps, have been attained by permitting the noble colonists (amongst whom the land had been apportioned) gradually to blend with the great mass of their new neighbours, and adopt the land as their own country. But, unhappily, through the influence of the Romish clergy, the course pursued only offered new stimulants to the mutual antipathy with which their relative circumstances had originally inspired the races. Thus, when the next male heir to the house of De Burgh seized the patrimonial estates of the Duchess of Clarence, he divided them amongst that clan, who forthwith adopted the laws, language, and manners of the native Irish, set the English Government at defiance, and transmitted the estates to their posterity. These particulars, apparently not directly connected with ecclesiastical matters, have to be mentioned, because the movement of the De Burghs led to the Parliament of Kilkenny passing several barbarous and severe laws for the future coercing the English settlers: they are called "the Statute of Kilkenny," and are well described as a declaration of perpetual war against the native Irish and all the English settlers who identified themselves with the Irish. The baneful effects of this impolitic measure continue to be felt to this day. The excuse for the enactment of these laws rests on the grant of Ireland to Henry II., and their being designed to the honour of God and his *glorious Mother*, and of the Holy Church; and the statute enjoins, that the civil power shall give due effect to the sentence of excommunication pronounced by the ecclesiastical authorities. Indeed, all the statutes under the Plantagenets were framed for the maintenance and authority of the Romish Church in Ireland, because it was by the influence of that Church that the State derived its power, and by the aid of the Romish clergy the Government, as then constituted, foolishly hoped to reconcile the Irish to English rule, though debarred of English privileges. Thus we find the statute extended so far as to forbid the English settlers acting as godfathers or godmothers to Irish families, or acting as foster-parents, and it even forbad the wearing of the Irish dress, or speaking the language.* Further, it was made highly penal to present a mere Irishman to an ecclesiastical benefice; or to receive him into a monas-

---

* The great animosity which has so long existed in Ireland against the Saxon name arose from the useless and impolitic measure of trying to force a new language on the Irish, at the same time stigmatizing their own to which they were fondly bound. Whatever assistance the Anglo-Norman Kings received in their expeditions against Ireland was not obtained from the Saxon part of the community, but from their own kindred, the ancient Britons, then settled in Wales.

tery or other religious house; or to entertain an Irish bard, minstrel, or story-teller; or to admit an Irish horse to graze on the pasture of an Englishman. Thus, the opportunity which, on this occasion, offered for the amalgamation and reconciliation of the two races was not only nationally lost, but the most taunting insults were offered to the best feelings of human nature. Everything Irish was denounced as an abhorrence to God and man, and the bitterness of civil strife was impregnated with the deadly poison of religious bigotry.

On this point it only remains to be noticed, that of the eight prelates, who attended the Parliament at Kilkenny when this statute was passed, no less than seven were of Papal appointment, and three of those were apostates from the Irish Church.

CHAPTER XV.

Wickliff.—State of the Clergy in England.—Lollards.—Henry IV.—His Policy.—Arundel.—Lord Cobham.—Public Commotions.—Reynold Pecock, Bishop of Chichester.—Art of Printing introduced into England.

THE period had now arrived when Wickliff, the great instrument whom the Most High destined should bring about his purposes of mercy towards the spiritually-enslaved English, appeared in active life. Through his means, Englishmen were enabled, during the reign of Richard II., to search the Scriptures for themselves in their native language; and, therefore, he may well be styled, the Phosphorus Match of the Reformation. We must now, however, revert a few years to state, that this remarkable man was born in the year 1324; he studied at, and became a member of the University of Oxford; and it appears, an awful pestilence which ravaged Europe about 1350 deeply impressed his mind. The rapacity and vices of the begging friars seem to have attracted first his attention, and then his consideration, whilst at Oxford, and against them he offered his earliest rebukes, in connexion also with the prevailing [A.D. 1356] disgraceful conduct of the regular clergy. His primary literary work appears to have been directed against the covetousness of the Court of Rome. The subject was well chosen, for covetousness is a vice so open to observation, and so palpably contrary to the precepts of the Gospel, that, although its existence proved nothing in reality against the doctrine of the Church, the discussion prepared men's minds to doubt whether infallibility of belief belonged to a body which was so evidently deficient in practice. The day of small things is not to be despised; God, who ordains all things for the best, made the examination of that Church's conduct the means of detecting the errors of her Creed. Wickliff was appointed Warden of Canterbury Hall by Simon de Islip, Archbishop of Canterbury; but was expelled by Langham the next year, when he succeeded to the Archiepiscopal chair.

[A.D. 1365.] About this time a demand was made by Urban V. for the arrears of the tribute conferred by John on the Papacy, and which had not been paid for some years. Wickliff publicly advocated the cause of the King and those who withheld it, and maintained the soundness of the answer sent by Parliament, that "as neither John, nor any other king, had power to dispose of his kingdom without the consent of the Parliament, no subsequent monarch could be bound by any such transfer, in itself illegal." Again, when Richard II. had come to the throne, Peter's pence, which appears to have been discontinued, was again claimed, and the subject having been discussed in Parliament, was referred to Wickliff, who maintained, that as an alms, or charitable donation, it might be lawful for the kingdom to suspend the payment, which had originally been made as a free gift. This, with his opposition to the power of binding and loosing, rendered him obnoxious to the Papal authority; while his constant strictures upon the infamous demands and unholy lives of the friars and ecclesiastic dignitaries exposed him to the hatred of many powerful Churchmen. But, by his translation of the Holy Scriptures, he let loose from its long Popish imprisonment that volume which alone can make men wise unto salvation. The Word of God was no longer "bound," and when, through his learning and exertion, that came forth to light and liberty, a new era commenced, the first-fruits whereof were exhibited by the martyrs of the Reformation, and are now written, not on the hearts of only British Protestants, but on those of all who faithfully desire to extend the Redeemer's kingdom by the influence of pure and undefiled religion. The close of this era is still hidden in futurity.

Gregory XI. issued several bulls, by which Simon Sudbury, Archbishop of Canterbury, and W. Courtney, Bishop of London, were appointed Papal Commissioners to try Wickliff on certain points brought against him. A bull had been previously sent against him to Oxford, but his tenets had taken such deep root in that place, that it produced little effect. Before, therefore, the above-mentioned Commissioners he appeared [A. D. 1377] in St. Paul's; but the presence of John of Gaunt, Duke of Lancaster, the Queen-mother, and others of the nobility, who warmly espoused his cause, operated so much to his advantage, that it not only stayed the proceedings on that occasion, but also at a subsequent meeting held at Lambeth.

The death of Gregory put an end to the Commission; but Wickliff's health now began to decline through anxiety and fatigue. During the next year he was brought nearly to the grave by a severe fever he laboured under at Oxford; and then his old enemies, the friars, in company with the aldermen of the city, visited him, and exhorted him as a dying man to do them justice for the many injuries which the society had experienced from him. Upon this he ordered himself to be raised in his bed, and exclaimed aloud, "I shall not die, but live, and declare the evil deeds of the friars." He recovered, and retired to his living of Lutterworth, preaching the truth, addressing the King, the people, and the Pope by his writings, expecting that, ere long, he should be subjected to personal suffering; this, in mercy to him, was not permitted, for his course was nearly run. He was seized with a fit of palsy when cited to appear before Urban, and was obliged to plead his infirmity and consequent inability to appear. The disorder shortly afterwards again [A. D. 1384] attacked him. During the time of Divine service in his parish church, he fell down and became speechless; and this circumstance has not failed to attract the notice of his enemies, who, in their writings, have recorded the event with Popish acrimony. Some of the errors and expressions which they have also imputed to him are so obviously absurd that they confute themselves. An apparently unfounded idea has also been mooted, that Wickliff was unsound as to belief in the doctrine of justification by faith and sanctification by the Holy Spirit. Authors, however, of undoubted credit, who seem to have investigated the subject, affirm that he was most distinct in his declarations with regard to both those doctrines, and that he directed his hearers to look up to Christ to be saved, and to seek the aid of the Holy Spirit to raise up even good thoughts within them; and that at the very time he was proceeding with all outward moderation in obviating false reports respecting his faith, he had prepared his own mind for extremities of the most fearful description. Perhaps, the greatest testimony as to the genuineness of his religion is the well-attested fact, that ultimately, the Pope (in accordance with a decree which had been passed by the Council of Constance in 1415,) directed, that as Wickliff had died an obstinate heretic, his bones should be dug up and flung on a dunghill. Fleming, Bishop of Lincoln, accordingly sent his officers to Lutterworth; his remains were by them taken up and burnt, and declaring that not only they should perish for ever, but his doctrines also, cast his ashes into the Swift, a brook which flows near the town. They were disappointed; for, as Fuller observes, "the Swift conveyed his ashes into the Avon—the Avon into the Severn—the Severn into the narrow seas—and they into the main ocean:" and thus the ashes of Wickliff were made the emblems of his doctrine, which has been dispersed all the world over. This decree against the remains of Wickliff was followed, in about six weeks, by the Council issuing another, forbidding the cup in the Sacrament of the Lord's Supper from being administered to the laity. Two or three claimants for the Popedom disturbed the peace of Europe, which, with the disputes in the General Councils, proved, that neither unity nor infallibility prevailed in the Romish Church. May it not here be asked, if Wickliff was not justified in protesting against Popery, and in calling upon his countrymen to shake off its yoke? For observe, the Pope had revived his claim of sovereignty over the realm. When he demanded the payment of the grant made by John, his revenues in the kingdom exceeded, by five times, those paid to the English monarch. The clergy, in spite of the law of mortmain, were possessed of one-half of the landed property in the kingdom; the monks and friars swarmed throughout the country, and beset the chambers of the weak and dying, and persuading them that there was no salvation without their passports to heaven, much of the property of the country fell into their hands by the bequests of their dupes, who impoverished their families under the false hope of saving their own souls. And now let the following warning of Wickliff be recorded, "God says that evil teachers are the cause of the destruction of the people." And further, let it be borne in mind that what has been may be. Was it not a time to cry, "Come out of her, my people?" And Wickliff did not do that till the ministers of the Romish Church had ceased to preach the words of eternal life, and made lying miracles, legendary histories, and puerile and monstrous fables of deliverance from purgatory, the subject of their pulpit discourses. His translation of the Scriptures, however, was his grandest movement towards the Reformation, and he multiplied copies of them as far as he could, and placed them [A.D. 1383] in the hands of Scripture-readers,[*] whom he sent forth to read out of the Book of Life, so that the men of England might hear them speak in their own tongues, wherein they were born, the wonderful works of God. Thus, as Dr. Lingard, the Roman Catholic historian, confesses, "a spirit of inquiry was generated, and the seeds were sown of that religious revolution, which, in little more than a century, astonished and convulsed the nations of Europe." Here, then, again, in our own land,[†] according to one hostile to Protestants, there was Protestantism in England before Luther existed! "The Scripture alone is truth!" "The Scripture alone is the faith of the Church!" This was Wickliff's

[*] Our Protestant forefathers. See — Gilly, D.D., Prebendary of Durham.
[†] See page 33, Alban.

argument;—" the grand and solid maxim," says his eloquent biographer, " upon which, as upon the Eternal Rock, he built up the defence of his great undertaking, and indeed his whole scheme of Reformation." We have here the vigorous germ of Protestantism cast by him, with a bold and vigorous hand, into the generous soil of his country, there to lie dormant and inert till the season should arrive for its starting into life.

[A.D. 1384.] The death of Wickliff checked, but did not crush the springing plant of the Reformation. His codes, his opinions, and his principles were circulated by his followers, who were called Lollards; why so called we cannot satisfactorily learn, further than that it was a designation, probably, of German origin, and given in England as a term of reproach. In spite of every attempt to keep them down, the Lollard Protestants increased in number, and they received the countenance of Ann of Bohemia, the consort of Richard II. The accounts of this excellent princess as regards religion are unhappily very brief; yet they merit our attention, because they seem to illustrate the course of Divine Providence in paving the way for that connexion between England and Bohemia, by which the labours of Wickliff became so serviceable in propagating the Gospel on the Continent through the means of John Huss and Martin Luther.

It is recorded of Ann that she had the Gospels in English, and when she died (A.D. 1394) Arundel, Archbishop of York, preached her funeral sermon; and dwelling on her excellences, particularly noticed that circumstance in her praise. The reader will therefore, doubtless, be surprised and mortified to find, that, shortly after the death of the good Queen Ann, this Prelate, to the utmost of his power, stirred up the King to harass and persecute even to death, throughout the kingdom, those who dared to read or study, in their native language, the Gospel of Jesus Christ. Such inconsistencies are not uncommon in the annals of human nature.

Many of the followers of Wickliff—henceforth to be spoken of as Lollards—refused, on scriptural grounds, accepting benefices, in consequence of the existing state of the English Church; and travelled, instead, through the country, diffusing the purer doctrines of Christianity. The Romanists, aware of the weakness of their cause, ordered an inquisitorial commission to be issued against all such as held what they termed heretical opinions, enjoining that search be made after them. But at that time the Lollards suffering little from it, presented a Petition to Parliament, in which, with severe animadversions, they represented the evils which existed in the Church.

[A. D. 1399.] The circumstances, however, by which Henry IV., surnamed Bolingbroke, came to the throne rendered it necessary for him to strengthen his interests with every species of ally, and there was no method by which the support of the Papal Church could be so easily gained as by assisting the bishops in their severities against the Lollards. To this cause do historians trace the statute which empowered the bishops to proceed against them; and, if incorrigible, to hand them over immediately to the secular power, which should forthwith "doom them to be burnt." What a Parliament! What a state of things! What a picture of Popery! Here is, however, no concealment. The object of the Bill was openly professed— "to burn heretics." The aid, therefore, of the clergy was bought at a price which will ever cover the name of Henry IV. (the son of John of Gaunt, the patron and protector of Wickliff) with infamy. With the true spirit of narrow-minded bigotry, those who kept the books and writings of Wickliff and the Lollards in their possession were specially subjected to punishment. The offenders, likewise, were not ascertained by common process at law, but by inquisitorial inquiries of the Romish bishops and clergy. When condemned by them, they were delivered to the magistrates to be burnt alive. In the examinations of these persons, of which several remain in their original forms in the bishops' registers, besides others, written soon after the examinations took place, great similarity prevails. The questions on which condemnation was pronounced, though varied, ordinarily turned on transubstantiation, or on submission to the authority of the Church. Thus it was reserved for the Romish Prelates, in the reign of Henry IV., to take advantage of the weakness of an usurper to make the civil powers their agents for putting to death men, who could say with the apostle Paul, (Acts xxiv. 14,) "After the way which they call heresy, so worship I the God of my fathers, believing all things which are written in the law and in the prophets." Arundel, who has been mentioned as favouring the knowledge of the Scriptures during the life of Ann, Queen of Richard II., was the chief promoter of the cruel law just described; and he immediately caused it to be put in force, by condemning William Sawtree, a priest of London, for refusing to worship the cross, and for asserting that the bread used in the sacrament continued to be bread after the priest pronounced over it the words of the Mass service. [A. D. 1401.] For these opinions William Sawtree was burnt alive—the first of the noble army of martyrs, who counted not their lives dear to them in resisting the errors of Popery. Romanists and some other writers attempt to gloss over those murders, by representing that the victims suffered as political offenders; but this representation will not avail. Burning to death was not the mode of executing criminals against the *State* in England; it was, moreover, a practice which had prevailed against heretics on the Continent during the two preceding centuries.

Popery and Protestantism * now fairly began to display their opposite characters in England, at the religious trials and examinations which henceforward became very frequent. But as various excellent publications † are in free circulation, which particularly detail them and recount the martyrdoms of the Protestant saints, they will only be generally alluded to in these pages, which are rather intended to set forth matters of importance in connexion with them which have hitherto been overlooked. We will, therefore, remark, that throughout these trials the Lollards cleared themselves of every reasonable suspicion of factious innovation.

They were chiefly known by their contempt and hatred of the Romish religion and of its ministers, joined to a determination to read the Scriptures, and other books relating to religion, in their own tongue. Occasionally these habits led some holy and undaunted

* Though the first ecclesiastical act which may come under that name may be dated as far back as the time of Irenæus, and of the Christians of Gaul, about the year of our Lord, 200; Claudius, Bishop of Turin, is allowed to be the one, through whom it was really introduced, about the year 817.

† "History of Lollards;" "Days of Queen Mary;" "Fox's History of Martyrs."

spirit to brave the horrors of the blazing pile; but more commonly were seen those, who, shrinking from this agonizing death, had abjured their opinions. Such unhappy Christians were branded on the cheek, and badged upon the shoulder. Nor were they allowed to go abroad with anything upon their heads, which might conceal the letter marked upon their cheek; nor without a dress on which a faggot was not worked, or painted, on the left shoulder. Others of the poor Lollards were confined in monasteries, nominally, as penitents, but really, as prisoners for life. Whatever may be the pretences of their personal enemies, and their traducers of the present day, it is clear that these individuals were perfectly void of political offence; and that spiritual error formed the only charge which could be brought against them. It is, therefore, clear that for the Gospel's sake alone they suffered.

The civil war, which first broke out in the reign of Henry IV., between the two rival houses of York and Lancaster, and which is styled the "War of the Roses," put a little check to religious inquiry and religious persecution, though it did not quite extinguish either; as the name of many a martyr in the cause of Christ is recorded in the page of ecclesiastical and general history.

Immediately after the coronation of Henry V. the persecuting Archbishop Arundel prepared himself again for the extermination of "heresy," (which, it seems, was daily becoming more prevalent in the kingdom,) by causing a Synod to be held at St. Paul's. [A.D. 1413.] The object of its assembling was, to repress the growth of the Gospel and, especially, to withstand the noble and worthy Lord Cobham. At this Synod appeared the twelve inquisitors, who had been appointed at Oxford the year before, to search after heretics and Wickliff's books. The offences of which Lord Cobham was charged were his maintenance of a great number of itinerant preachers in many parts of the country; his care in collecting, transcribing, and circulating the works of Wickliff amongst the common. people; and, more especially, his zeal in having copies of Wickliff's Bible multiplied at great expense to himself. The particulars of the accusations of heresy, and of his examination, are preserved. He appears to have been condemned by the cruel bigotry of his enemies; but he contrived to escape from the Tower, and fled into Wales, where he was concealed for four years. Arundel and the Romish party sought to retain their influence over the mind of the King (who, it was conjectured, was favourably disposed to Lord Cobham,) by pretending that a rebellion was contemplated, and that many thousands were assembling in St. Giles's-fields, headed by that nobleman: whereas he was yet a fugitive in Wales; and the thousands numbered at most about 100 persons, secretly met together for the purpose of religious worship. Through the means of Lord Powis, Cobham was apprehended in Wales, and sent by him a prisoner to London. [A.D. 1417.] His death was not long delayed. He was dragged upon a hurdle, with insult and barbarity, to St. Giles's-fields, and there hanged in chains upon a gallows, and a fire being kindled underneath, he was slowly burnt to death.

Arundel had died in A.D. 1414, and was succeeded in his See by Henry Chichely, who continued Archbishop of Canterbury till April, 1443. He was more violent than his predecessor; and, by means of banishment, forced abjurations, and the flames, the vestiges of godliness were well-nigh effaced from the land.*

[A.D. 1432.] Henry VI., now on the throne of England, proved a mere puppet in the hands of others; being the slave of superstition, and enfeebled in his reason and understanding. Moreover, civil discord prevailed, and the glory which England had acquired in France had passed its meridian. A country girl was the feeble instrument appointed to discomfit the English princes and warriors, and to commence a new course, which rolled back on their own land the tide of sufferings they had carried thither. The wars of the Roses also distracted the nation, and divided the kingdom under the banners of the two contending parties. The house of Lancaster, supported in its usurpations by the Church of Rome, was compelled to be at enmity with all who, politically or religiously, differed from her; and all the cruel severities exercised at this time upon those who differed from the Romish Church only increased the opposition and hatred against the ruling powers. Persecution for conscience' sake always defeats itself in the end, though for a time it may seem to prevail.

Accordingly, we find that discontents broke out; tumultuous assemblies were held; the ruling ecclesiastics loudly called for unity: this, in their acceptation of the term, meant blind submission in spiritual, as well as temporal, matters; but the measures

* This Archbishop built a prison, mostly used for the clergy suspected of heresy. In an upper room at the top of that tower which is still called the Lollards' Tower there yet remains some iron rings, to which the prisoners were fastened, and on the walls may be seen some written memorials of those who were confined there.

resorted to by them for this purpose only caused the national discontent to be still greater. There had been a cause for these inflictions. The truth had been perverted in the land, and the fatal result proceeded according to the words spoken by the prophet: "Woe unto them that call evil good, and good evil; that put darkness for light, and light for darkness; that put bitter for sweet, and sweet for bitter." The prophetic declaration adds: "Shall I not visit for these things, saith the Lord; and shall not my soul be avenged on such a nation as this?"

[A. D. 1450.] While these circumstances were progressing, no small stir was occasioned among the Romish hierarchy in England; for one of their own number, Reynold Pecock, Bishop of Chichester, though he did not entirely adopt the views of the Lollards, would not join in the cruel means used to extirpate them; and because he advocated the general reading of the Scriptures by the laity, was first expelled the House of Lords, (A. D. 1457,) and then deprived of his bishopric. (A. D. 1458.) He was detained a prisoner for life in Thorney Abbey, Cambridgeshire, where some assert he was brought to an untimely end. So great, however, was the general opposition to everything that had the appearance of reformation, that error and superstitious rites were multiplied by the clergy, rather than diminished. It has been well observed, that "at the time when all the Christian world was brought under the Church of Rome; when deliverance seemed not only past the power, but also past the hope of man; in this very time, so dangerous, and so desperate, when man's power could do no more—then "the blessed wisdom and Omnipotent power of God began to work for his Church; not with warlike weapons, but with printing, writing, and reading—severally destined to dispel darkness by light, error by truth, ignorance by learning, and thus to accomplish his purposes. As before related, the Scriptures had been translated into English by Wickliff. Now, about the latter end of Edward IV.'s reign, it being the Lord's appointed time, the art of printing was introduced into England, and it dealt an effectual blow at ignorance and superstition.

Knowledge always brings in its train rebellion against superstition. Thus, printing, at this period, was the special instrument of the Most High, in behalf of his persecuted Church, and became, like the power imparted by the influence of the Holy Ghost in the gift of tongues, the messenger of the doctrine of the Gospel to all nations and to all countries under heaven.

CHAPTER XVI.

Remarks on the Reign of Henry VII.—Rebellion in Ireland, and the Nature of a Romish Oath.—Henry VIII. ascends the Throne of England.—Disputes with the Pope.—Shakes off the Supremacy of the Pope.—Persecutions.—Suppression of Monasteries, &c., &c., &c.—Bad Policy respecting Ireland.

WITH the exception of continued tales of persecution against the Lollards, the reigns of Edwards IV. and V. present so very little matter for the subject of these pages, that, passing them over, we will proceed at once to state, that when Richard III. took possession of the English throne he found a formidable competitor for the same, and one before whom he fell, in the head of the Lancastrian party, viz., Henry Tudor, the son of the Earl of Richmond, and Margaret of Beaufort. [A.D. 1485.] As Henry VII., this descendant of John of Gaunt paid little attention to ecclesiastical matters of any description, and accordingly we have merely to record, that, as regards religion, the gloomy season of this reign tended to check and obscure its immediate growth and outward prosperity in these realms; and that the attachment of sincere and believing Christians to their living Head could only be manifested by the badge of persecution which they bore throughout it. It is one, however, which can never be mistaken, inasmuch as hypocrites never subject themselves to its final ordeal and penalties, and, therefore, the existence of the Church of Christ can alone be traced by the martyrs' blood, which stains the page of England's history during the period referred to. The foundation of their faith, and the increasing influence of the Bible, whereon it rested, can, however, be clearly read by the light of the fires which consumed them, and which likewise imbued with increased determination and resolution, the hearts and minds of many of those who witnessed their sufferings and their constancy. Meanwhile, the divided state of public opinion encouraged the Romish Hierarchy, who had, for some time, remained politically inactive, to appear in open rebellion against the united authority of both King and Pope.

Though Henry VII.'s title to the Crown had been acknowledged by the Pope, the Irish bishops, with the exception of four, and a proportionate number of the clergy, joined in the well-known conspiracy formed to dethrone him, and received the stripling Simnel, the creature of an obscure ecclesiastic at Oxford, with an extravagant affectation of loyal zeal, and proceeded to place him on the throne of the Plantagenets, by putting, in Christ Church, Dublin, a crown on his head, which had hitherto adorned a statue of the Virgin Mary.

[A. D. 1486.] When the bishops had carried their treason to the last extremity, they began to be visited with the same misgivings as in the case of Edward Bruce. To soften the displeasure of the Pope, they sent him a subsidy; yet, in spite of this, they would have been excommunicated, and have felt the full weight of Papal anger, if Henry VII., the monarch against whom they had rebelled, had not interposed, and admitted them to pardon, by accepting their proffered oaths of allegiance; and a suitable officer was sent over to receive the same. The attempt made by these men to elude the force of these tendered oaths of their fidelity exhibits a strong instance of that detestable casuistry, by which schoolmen of the Church of Rome have seared the natural susceptibility of conscience. When every difficulty respecting these oaths of their allegiance appeared to be adjusted, it was demanded by Kildare, the leader of the aforesaid rebellion, that the Host should be consecrated by one of his own chaplains. This demand involved literally "the mystery of iniquity," which the proposer could never have fathomed for himself, and which few Roman Catholic laymen of the present day would be able to comprehend without a particular explanation; and in the hope of extending the knowledge of the deceptious nature of a Popish oath amidst those now entering upon the affairs and duties of life, and thereby warning and guarding them against the same mischief in these days, it shall now be given at length, according to the distinguished author of the present day, from whom so much has been gathered up in this volume as precious seed for the future:—

"It has long been a doctrine of the Papal Church, republished at Trent under the sanction of a curse on all who deny it, that the *intention* of the *officiating priest* is necessary for the validity of a religious rite. The conspirators were assured that the intention of Kildare's chaplain would be cordially in their favour; thus, the form of consecration would be the juggling illusion of a mountebank; the wafer would be no host, and the protestation made upon it, 'so help me this holy Sacrament of God's body in form of bread, *here present* to my salvation or damnation,' however awful in its terms, would have no meaning, and consequently, no terrors to those whom the prelate should initiate into so comfortable a secret. On such an occasion as that mentioned above, the dogma will encourage the unprincipled villain; but to the honestly superstitious it abounds with consequences the most alarming. A priest cannot know if he is lawfully called to the ministry; his people are equally ignorant, whether his ministerial acts are valid; the want of intention in himself, or in the bishop who ordained him, is sufficient to invalidate all he does. Thus, a matron can never be sure that she is married; or a devotee, that he has received any one of those sacraments, which he, at the same time, believes to be indispensable to his salvation. All this is unaccountable in a Church which maintains her own infallibility, *in order to save her votaries from doubt*, or rather, it would be unaccountable did it not teach the necessity of being always on good terms with the priesthood." The words of the Trent decree are these: 'If any one shall say that there is not required in ministers, when they consecrate and administer the sacraments, an *intention* of doing what *the Church* does, let him be anathema.'" (Sess. vi., canon 9.) *

Edgecombe, Henry VII.'s Commissioner on this occasion, was aware of the perfidy of the demand, and insisted that the Mass should be celebrated by his own chaplain; and history possesses a description of the whole ceremony, which shows the appalling character of the premeditated prevarication. The bishops, however, had another evasion in reserve, *the benefits of which did not extend to their less favoured lay associates.* The oaths of the *prelates* were followed by a sweeping

* The Council of Trent was the last held in the Church of Rome, and its decrees are received implicitly by Romanists at the present day.

clause of exception, "Salvo ordine episcopali," saving the privileges of their order; privileges, of which themselves were the only judges, and before the sacred inviolability of which all secular rights and all secular obligations were required to give way. Let any one study the Word of God while he yet lingers o'er the practical exhibition of error and knavery just detailed, and on which it was pretended the religious creed which produced such fruit was built, and the necessity of the Reformation is at once placed before him in the clearest light. In further meditating on the steps which have thus led us onwards, even to the dawn of the Reformation, (but in the twilight of which we shall still abide, and shall not emerge from during the entire reign of Henry VIII.,) we must not be induced to lay too much stress on the individual merit or sufferings of those who have already, or may hereafter, be necessarily brought forward and represented as pioneers in the cause of truth. Grossetête and Bradwardine, Wickliff and Pecock, Sawtree and Cobham, with many, very many, whose names have reached us,* and some whose names have not, and are alone known to the Lord, may and did advance that blessed principle amongst our forefathers. Those, however, who will behold the truth in these past events, must look beyond all these human instruments to their great Artificer. Truly they were individually led by him, and lent their brightness to dispel the thick darkness which enveloped this land; but we shall fail to derive from the study of our ecclesiastical history its greatest advantage, if we turn not our mental eyes to that

* Accounts may be read of them in the "History of the Lollards," "Fox's Book of Martyrs," &c., &c.

Omnipotent and Eternal brightness, which no human device can extinguish, and look not up to the true Church of Christ, built on the Rock of Truth, against which the gates of hell shall never prevail. The Reformation was at hand, and the dark ages had nearly reached their close, when Henry VII. died; but, as splendid cathedrals and abbeys then adorned the land, chapels and colleges had been built and endowed, and the Romish clergy persecuted and destroyed their falsely-named heretics with impunity, the most intelligent amongst them were, probably, little prepared for that event, when Henry VIII. succeeded him as England's Sovereign. As Protestants, Britons have too long suffered Romanists to state, that to Henry VIII. we owe the glorious event distinguished amongst us by the name of the Reformation. We have, indeed, too tamely permitted this assertion to press like an incubus on the bosom of our religion: let us now throw off the weight, and cast it back on them whose religious nurseling Henry was. The Reformation, as a spiritual movement, was never engendered in his mind. Men had begun to think seriously on matters of faith long before his reign had commenced, and the progress of free inquiry and scriptural knowledge advanced in spite of him, rather than in consequence of his aid and protection. Protestantism, as a principle, had, moreover, firmly taken root downward, and was bearing fruit upward in this land before he appeared on the throne. Henry gave, perhaps unwittingly, an impulse to the political engine that first shook Popery from its commanding position in this country, and struck down the Papal arm when directed against himself; yet it is notorious in history, that it was an individual, as well as a political motive, and not a religious one, which induced the quarrel between himself and the Pope.

Before proceeding further into the ecclesiastical events of Henry VIII.'s reign, we must offer a few remarks on a simultaneous religious movement which was progressing amongst the Continental Churches, and which it would have been unnecessary to have here noticed, but that it has been misrepresented by its being set forth by some historians, that Luther's opinions produced the British, as well as the Continental, Reformation. Let us only revert to past events in this land, when the reverse will appear to be the case. It is a well authenticated fact, that the Bohemian nobles in attendance on Anne, the pious consort of Richard II., took back with them to their native land Wickliff's Bible, as well as his own theological writings, which became the blessed means of enlightening the eyes of many of their countrymen. Amongst others, John Huss and Jerome of Prague stand forth most conspicuous; for it led to their martyrdom. Eventually the writings of John Huss fell into the hands of Luther, who likewise soon adopted and promulgated the opinions of the same *early English Reformer;* the result of which is so well known from details in mere secular histories, that it need not be here entered upon: enough has been stated in the foregoing few lines to establish the fact, that Luther trimmed the bright lamp wherewith he illumined the Christian hemisphere of Europe with the oil of Divine truth, drawn from the English vessels, borne hence by the Bohemian nobles, rather than that our Reformers of the sixteenth century lighted theirs at the German's torch. Luther's first-published attack on the Romish

Church appeared in the year 1516; and those who avowed their confession of faith in accordance with Luther's opinion, as a public body, adopted or assumed the Latin name of Witnesses—Protestants, at the second diet of Spires, A.D. 1529, when six princes and fourteen imperial cities protested against the intolerance of the Popish majority.* †

In returning to the immediate subject of this volume, we must remark, that when the Reformation first occupied the minds of Englishmen more generally, and began to assume, therefore, a national character, the conformity of its doctrines to those of Scripture became an object of deserving solicitude, yet was one, few persons had the means of solving. To remedy this defect, there was no want of zeal or talents amongst those who desired to see their country blessed with a change of religion; but the King was so little inclined to favour their views, that he issued a proclamation against Tyndal's English translation, which had been published at Antwerp, A.D. 1526, declaring that the possession of the book, after thirty days, would expose the person convicted of having it to the penalty of heresy—"the flames." And this proclamation was undoubtedly carried into effect; for an old man, named Thomas Harding, of Buckinghamshire, having his house searched, a New Testament was found. The man was burnt alive, and all who carried a faggot to his stake had an indulgence of forty days granted to them. ‡

* See Appendix, No. I.
† Claudius, Bishop of Turin, is sometimes mentioned as the first Protestant Bishop, A.D. 817.
‡ For a full account of these martyrdoms, the reader is referred

While the Cardinal Archbishop Wolsey, then in Royal favour, lived, no public recognition of the duty of putting the English translation of the Scriptures into the hands of the people could be expected. That Cardinal Archbishop, who held, by Papal dispensation, at one time the revenues of four bishoprics,* hated even the art of printing; but eventually the clergy began to suspect that it might prove above their power to prevent the Scriptures from circulating in English, and they changed their outward and acknowledged endeavours to restrain men from reading them, merely attacking Tyndal's edition; and, in the Star Chamber, a promise was made, that the Scriptures should speedily be more faithfully translated; but the pledge not being redeemed, the people, in spite of every precaution and tyranny used to prevent it, continued to supply themselves with copies from the Netherlands.

Henry, however, more conspicuously appeared on the stage of life as the champion of the Romish religion, by attacking Luther in a treatise which he wrote, entitled, "An Assertion of the Seven Sacraments," and thereby so far obtained for himself the approval and favour of the Pope, that he declared that Henry should be styled in future, "The Defender of the Faith:" a designation which had been borne by Richard II. When, however, Henry desired to rid himself of his consort, Catharine of Arragon, an idea which the former practices of the See of Rome had encouraged him in; and which the opinion of his

to Fox's "Book of Martyrs;" "The History of the Lollards;" published by the Religious Tract Society.

* Some few years since it was stated in Parliament that pluralities were first held by Protestant clergy. Could ignorance or knavery have induced the assertion?

confessor, Longchamp, Bishop of London, and Wolsey, the Chancellor of England and Archbishop of York, together with all the prelates, (with the exception of Fisher, Bishop of Rochester,) not only confirmed, but further strengthened, by pronouncing his marriage with her of doubtful validity, he not only fearlessly cast off the Popish yoke himself, but legalized resistance to the Pope's supremacy throughout the wide circuit of his realms. In the hour, however, when he most depended upon Wolsey's support, that prelate deserted his cause, and tried by intriguing policy to carry forth the views of the Pope, who was constrained to advocate the cause of Charles V., Emperor of Germany, who interfered in behalf of his aunt, Catharine. The clergy generally, as well as both the Universities of England, continued stedfast to the opinion they had formed and publicly avowed, that the marriage was not a legal one; and, therefore, sanctioned the desirability of a divorce. Wolsey's policy did not save him; it led to his disgrace, and, in the end, to his downfall, as he suffered in consequence of his intrigues, respecting the affairs of the English monarch with the Pope, under the law of Præmunire, which has already been described,* and was passed in the reign of Edward III., the provisions of which were further explained and extended under Richard II. The penalties and consequences of this measure so affected Wolsey, that he speedily sank beneath the weight of them, and died.

It may here be remarked that about the year A.D. 1515, long before Henry's dispute with the Pontiff, Cardinal Wolsey, with the sanction of the Pope, had suppressed forty monasteries, to increase the revenues

---

* See page 167.

of the Cardinal's new College at Oxford, and thereby
set Henry an example he afterwards acted upon.

Previous to, and whilst these events were taking
place, the overruling providence of the Almighty had
been guarding, guiding, and training the celebrated
Anne Boleyn, for her future exalted situation and
destiny; amidst the courtly circles of the exemplary
and pious princess, Claudia of Brittany, Consort of
Francis I. and his sister, Margaret, Duchess of
Alençon, both early favourers of the Reformation. She
returned to her native land, predisposed to favour the
Protestants of England, when the unregenerate and un-
subdued will of Henry placed her on its throne as his
Queen. [A.D. 1533.] The assistance which the learned
and pious Cranmer had rendered the monarch in this
affair, and his resistance likewise to the power of the
Pope, raised him happily about the same period to the
Primatical chair of Canterbury. When Anne gave
birth to Elizabeth, one of the most distinguished
of Britain's sovereigns, the Papal authority was
ominously, daily falling into more and more contempt.
Acts of Parliament were passed to restrain all payments
and appeals to the Pope, as a means for barring his
interference in English affairs. Clement, who then
bore that title, threatened to excommunicate Henry;
but the Papacy received a further blow from the convocation, and the two Universities deciding that *the
Bishop of Rome has no more power over England conferred on him by God's Word than any other bishop,*
orders were given to erase the Pope's name from all
books of devotion.

In reference to Ireland, we must state, that, Henry
had no sooner prevailed on the Lords and Commons of
England to renounce their spiritual obedience to the

Romish see and to acknowledge his supremacy instead, than, as a natural consequence, he proceeded to establish it in Ireland. Kildare, the head of the disaffected Geraldine party alluded to in the last reign, seems to have stood almost alone in opposing this present monarch; for no sooner had Henry asserted his claim to the entire sovereignty (1533) than we read that the nobles arrayed themselves on the side of the Crown. They forthwith abolished the title of "Lord," the only one the Pope had permitted to be assumed by the sovereigns of Britain, and proclaimed Henry King of Ireland, and supreme head of the Church on earth. Observe, this unanimity was not confined to that portion of the nobility which conformed to English customs and shared in the administration, but extended even to those powerful and refractory chieftains, who, having hitherto maintained a dubious struggle against the utmost force of the State, now came forward with rival zeal for the honour of royalty, and with the strongest professions of undivided allegiance. This conduct of the great lords was emulously imitated from the remotest regions of the north and south. All the most turbulent heads of the Irish tribes,—all those of the old English who had *adopted* the *Irish manners*, and had lived for ages in rude independence, and thereby earned for themselves the title of "Rebels," vied with one another in declarations of fidelity to the King, and executed their indentures in the amplest forms of submission. In these deeds, after due attention to civil affairs, they pledge themselves, as far as lieth in their power, to annihilate the usurped primacy and authority of the Bishop of Rome, &c., &c., &c. So far from any force being used in this religious change, it is recorded for the first time in her annals, that "Ireland was now at peace under one acknowledged sovereign;" and this is the more remarkable as being in open defiance of the Vatican. Further, when, eight years after, Paul III. issued the bull, in which he not only dethroned Henry, but pronounced him infamous; cut off from Christian burial; and doomed him to eternal curse and damnation; requiring war to be made on him, and those defending him to be seized and be made slaves,—we find the interval alluded to had not been misused or spent in idleness by the Pontiff; for lost chronicles had meanwhile been discovered in which Ireland was called the Holy Island; but all appeals, whether to superstition, to prophecy,* or to enthusiasm, proved unsuccessful: it was too obvious that the opposition of Rome and its partizans to Henry was nothing more than a struggle for *temporal* dominion, and not a sword was drawn in the quarrel of the ecclesiastics during the reigns of Henry and of his son Edward.†

In England, Henry's vigorous efforts to rid himself and his subjects of the Pope's supremacy were not received in so quiet a manner: and the same can be easily accounted for; as it is impossible to suppose that the steps he took towards a final separation of her Church from that of Rome, when she was to re-assume her primitive position, and once more step forth as a distinct and independent body, should have been acceptable to the great mass of those clergy whose

* The Pope signified that he had lately found an ancient prophecy of one St. Lazerianus, an Irish Archbishop of Cashel, which said, that the Church of Rome shall surely fall when the Catholic faith is once overthrown in Ireland, &c., &c., &c., adding to his exhortation to suppress heresy—"You see that when the Roman faith perisheth in Ireland, the See of Rome is fated to utter destruction."

† See Appendix, No. VI.

privileges and powers were thus directly attacked. Almost all the Bishops, as well as both the Universities, took the oath of the King's supremacy without hesitation. Bishops Bonner and Gardiner, who afterwards became, in Mary's time, the strongest advocates for the resumption of the Papal supremacy, were amongst the number. Those who were attached to the Romish cause artfully did so, hoping thereby to secure an influence over the monarch whose religious principles, they were too well aware, leaned towards those in which he had been educated, and to which he unhappily remained attached to the last.

The secret machinations of the monks and friars, who took advantage of the ordeal of confession, whereby every domestic and public feeling is wrung from the heart, were insidiously applied by them for the purpose of undermining the King's supremacy; which, added to the most blasphemous denunciations being issued against him from some of the pulpits, at length rendered it necessary for him to interfere. The King at first permitted the refractory friars to escape with a reprimand, but eventually many suffered the penalty of the law as traitors.

In 1535 the Parliament again renewed their former solicitations for a repeal of the Act against the Lollards; complaining of the cruelty of some of the prelates and their officers in calling men before them and accusing them of heresies; but refusing to state the name of their accusers, and obliging them to declare their opinions, and then condemning them for their words thus extorted. They succeeded in the partial repeal of this law of Henry IV., enacting instead, that heretics should not be taken up unless accused by two witnesses, and that they should be tried in open court.

The bigoted Papists were much troubled at these relenting measures, and being therefore desirous of embarrassing the reforming party, who aimed at a complete abrogation of those oppressive statutes, countenanced the impostures of the nun, Ann Barton, often called "the maid of Kent."

If her pranks and impostures had only maintained a harmless character all might have been passed over, or only slightly punished; but when her influence was used to proclaim the King's death within a month, in all which she was unaccountably supported by Fisher, Bishop of Rochester, and Sir Thomas More, the nun and her more immediate confederates were taken up and examined before the Council, when they confessed the whole imposture and plot. It is not required that the particulars should be here detailed, for they are fully treated of in histories of only a secular character. It being clearly demonstrated that she was a mere tool in the hands of the Papists, she and six of her accomplices were committed to the Tower on the charge of treason, where they remained till the meeting of Parliament, when they were properly tried, condemned, and executed as traitors at Tyburn. The nun and her confederates, with others who suffered for their crimes or political offences, are called martyrs by Romish historians; though it is clear that they underwent the death of traitors, or aggressors against the civil law, and not that of those who suffered on account of their religion. Amongst the limited number of those who cannot be charged with practising an unholy dissimulation in respect of the oath of supremacy, we find the names of Fisher, Bishop of Rochester, and Sir Thomas More, both great men and leading characters, and who had, in virtue of their respective offices, bitterly persecuted the Lollards; they now, in their turn, tasted the bitter cup of suffering. They honestly refused to take the oath referred to, and were attainted expressly on that account. They were tried and condemned—not by the bishops and their officers—but by the judges upon a verdict of a jury, after having been arraigned in the ordinary courts of law, and having pleaded not guilty to their indictment, which set forth that they denied the King's supremacy. The reader is again urged to notice the manner of death inflicted on these exalted individuals, for they fell beneath that appointed for traitors; thus their case is exhibited as clearly different to the martyrdoms of the Lollards. These remarks are not made with any design to speak lightly of their fate; but to set the truth before the reader, which, in matters at all connected with our Church history, is particularly needed at this time, because Romanists are making great exertions to restore the lost ascendancy of their sect. As one step towards the attainment of this object, they employ the historian's pen to misrepresent the character of individuals suspected of having been opposed to their creed, and to suppress or distort political facts militating to the disadvantage or discredit of the same.

Henry's quarrel with Rome was, in fact, against the Pope, and not against the errors of Romanism, to which he continued firmly attached. How can this be doubted, and he represented as the regal patron of the Reformation, when we find him issuing a proclamation in the year 1536 threatening death without mercy to all who denied or disputed the doctrine of transubstantiation or any other rites or ceremonies of the

Church of Rome—such as holy bread, holy water, processions, kneeling at and creeping to the cross on Good Friday, and similar superstitions?

Several Dutch and German Anabaptists as well as English Lollards were about this time committed to the flames, and the Popish religion still maintained its ground in England, excepting that the violence of persecution was a little abated by the influence of Queen Anne Boleyn, assisted by Cranmer and Cromwel. We further find that Cranmer interfered in behalf of the princess Mary, who, blindly attached to the authority of the Pope, refused to take the oath of supremacy; and her incensed father would have sent her to the Tower, to be tried and dealt with as a subject, had not Cranmer interposed and persuaded the offended monarch to the contrary. Yes, reader, the bigoted and cruel Queen Mary owed her life to Cranmer, and twenty years afterwards she paid her debt of gratitude by ordering him to be burnt alive. Popish writers conceal this fact respecting Cranmer, and unhappily their plan is followed by some of the leading authors of the present day, who endeavour to render the Reformers of our Church, whether sovereigns or subjects, contemptible: shading some characters with the false colouring of Romish prejudice, and then highly touching up their favourites with the bright tints of Romish and latitudinarian partiality, thereby leaving a false representation of them on the minds of the unthinking or superficial reader.

The refusal of the monks and friars (amongst whom we must especially enumerate the Prior and Monks of the Charter-house) to take the oath of the King's supremacy led to Cromwel's being appointed Vicar-General, and afterwards Lord-Vicegerent, for the special purpose of carrying into effect an order for the visitation of the monasteries. One of the first points, however, which fell under the cognizance of this new office was an inquiry into the authority from which the bishops derived their right to ecclesiastical jurisdiction. The Romish Church held that this was communicated from Christ through his vicar, the Pope, an idea which must give the Bishops of Rome an influence over the countries of Christendom, for which there is not the slightest foundation in Scripture. Henry, wishing to put an end to this error, now suspended all the bishops from the use of their episcopal authority during the visitation which he purposed to institute.*

After a time the power of exercising it was restored by a Commission, and there was no opposition raised on the part of the bishops, but on that of Gardiner. When the suspension was taken off they resumed the usual duties of their office. Ever since Augustine's time the increasing desire of power in the Papacy had led to the policy of its trying to keep the clergy of England, by enforcing celibacy, as distinct as possible from the rest of the people;† which measure, while it necessarily exposed

---

* Cromwel was probably selected for this office from his having been employed on a former and similar occasion by Cardinal Wolsey, when he suppressed, with the Pope's sanction, forty monasteries for the endowment of Christ Church College, Oxford.

† How different during those centuries (and is still) the policy of Rome in trying to withdraw the clergy from all domestic intercourse with the mass of the people, and thereby preventing, their respective interests from amalgamating, to that of our primitive forefathers, who, at the earliest date of our national records, are found to have not only wisely permitted them to associate with the other classes of society, but to have secured their presence and co-operation on every suitable occasion. Their interests were thereby then bound up

them to various temptations, and equally lowered them in general estimation, did not fail to direct all their energies towards the aggrandisement and enrichment of that particular society to which they severally belonged, yet every one of which was integrally bound to that power: monks have therefore been styled the Pope's Militia. The property, moreover, which specially belonged to the monasteries had been acquired through the subtle medium of confession and absolution, operating under the erroneous doctrine of purgatory. The greater part of the possessions of the monasteries had thus been obtained by the monks and friars belonging to them hovering round the death-beds of individuals, and persuading them to bestow their lands upon monastic orders, so that their souls might be prayed out of purgatory. This they accordingly did, leaving their families in poverty.* The learned Erasmus, who was also a monk, confirms this account, describing the way in which these confessors encouraged men in vicious conduct while alive, and then beset their death-beds.

The Commissioners made reports of their proceedings during their visitations of the monasteries, the

with that of the nation. Papacy and the narrow-mindedness of the dark ages withdrew and separated them; and, reader, you have the consequences portrayed in England's blood-stained pages from the Norman conquest to the period when the Reformation and its attendant blessings were nationally secured to us.

* Some years ago it was estimated that the rents of the lands formerly belonging to the Abbey of Glastonbury alone, exceeded three hundred thousand pounds per annum; it would now probably amount to half-a-million. Thus the influence of the Abbot, then and now, would be equal to that of a land-holder whose rent-roll amounted to half-a-million.

greater part of which, as well as other documents* of vast importance, were destroyed by Bonner and his associates, during the reign of Queen Mary; but a few remain which are sufficient to fill the mind of the reader with horror. In the foregoing pages it has been noticed that when Henry determined to throw off the dominion of Rome, the Irish, but more especially the true native Irish, warmly and eagerly went with him in the separation, and that not a sword was drawn by them in behalf of the opposing ecclesiastics. It is lamentable, therefore, to have to state, that all the advantages likely to have accrued from this disposition working in the hearts of the people were irretrievably lost; and the seeds of future disquiet (for now three hundred years) cast amongst them by the ill-judged policy of the fitful and unsteady Henry, permitting an Act to be passed, entitled "An Act for the English order, habit, and language," &c., &c. It contained likewise various enactments against the Irish dress, style of wearing their hair, &c., &c., all of which must have been most irksome. Then it went on still more unwisely to provide, "that spiritual promotion should be given only to such persons as could speak the

* In the reign of Queen Mary, Bonner, Cole, and Martin were appointed Commissioners, with power to examine the records of the preceding reigns, in order to search for all things which were done against the authority of the Pope, or concerning the examinations of the abbeys, that further orders might be given about them. Many important documents were then destroyed; for as Burnet says, "lest they should have been afterwards confessors, it was resolved they should be martyrs," *i. e.*, burnt! Some documents escaped this destruction, and by a singular oversight the Commission above alluded to, which was amongst the number, remains to this day.

English language, unless when such persons could not be had." It is ordered, that every archbishop and bishop, at the time of the admission of any person to spiritual promotion, " should administer an oath to the person promoted, that he would endeavour himself to learn and to teach the English tongue to all under his rule and government, and should keep, or cause to be kept, a school to learn English." The objection to this last enactment was not so much against the speaking or teaching the English language, but to the utter neglect and disuse of the Irish—one result of which was to leave their own much-loved language to the special use and advantage of Romish priests and services.*

How just and forcible are Dean Murray's observations on this statute,—" Had the great enemy of truth been the concoctor of these enactments no surer means could have been devised to arrest the progress of the Reformation." For, true it is, that this shuffling effort wherewith the proud heart of man has so often endeavoured to evade the mental curse imposed by the Lord himself on Noah's posterity, when they raised the standard of rebellion on the plains of Shinar, and whereby He scattered their tribes " abroad on the face of all the earth," has never been responded to by any of them. The attempt has ever failed, and the experience of centuries now proves, that to civilize, Christianize, and Protestantize a people, they must be approached through the softening and soothing medium of their native tongue. If the Lord's blighting denunciation had been withdrawn from amidst the wandering families of the Gentiles, wherefore began the Apostles on the day of Pentecost " to speak with other tongues as the Spirit

* See Appendix, No. VI.

gave them utterance?" Wherefore was a miracle performed which led the Gentile multitude, assembled on that memorable day, to say one to another, "Behold, are not all these Galileans? and how hear we every man in our own tongue wherein we were born"—but that the Lord knew, that without the gift of tongues the Apostles could not obey his command and preach the Gospel to every creature.

CHAPTER XVII.

Observations on Destruction of Monasteries.—Pope excommunicates and denounces Henry.—Bible Translated.—Romish Policy towards Henry.—Consequent Death of Cromwel.—Act of Six Articles passed.—King's Book published.—Persecutions arising therefrom.—Machinations of the Romish Party, and Martyrdoms of Protestants alluded to.—Death of Henry.—His Character.—General Observations, and Conclusion.

ROMAN Catholics and even Protestants sometimes assert, that since the destruction of the monasteries there has been a great increase of the poor in England. This is altogether a misstatement, as many documents still exist of an earlier date, which testify to the contrary. In confirmation of this we will first notice, that in A.D. 1516, Sir Thomas More wrote his first edition of his "Utopia," and that therein he speaks of the increase of beggary, and states that many persons, wealthy abbots themselves among them, converted large tracts into sheep-walks for the profit of the wool, &c., &c.; and, as a remedy, Sir Thomas proposed, that "the beggars should be placed in the convents of the Benedictine monks, since it was owing, in a great measure, to the advance of those wealthy abbeys that the number of mendicants so much increased." Let the reader bear in mind, that the great increase of beggars and the progressive impoverishment of the land here alluded to, took place before the Reformation, and was attributed by a zealous Romanist to the multiplication of monastic establishments. This statement is confirmed by an Act of Parliament passed in the year A.D. 1534, which also attributes the increase of the poor to the same causes as those mentioned by Sir Thomas More, and says, they are thereby "driven to fall to theft, to the utter destruction and desolation of the realm." Yet, when the most prominent treatise on the subject came out, in 1526, Sir T. More wrote against it in utter contradiction to his former published opinions. The reader ought again to notice, that the indigent members of society in those days had no poor-laws to appeal to, when the hour of want and distress overtook them; and that provision for the poor of England subsequently emanated from the policy of that Queen and her ministers, who likewise secured the principles of the Reformation to our national Church. The treatise just alluded to was written in the form of a Petition, and was entitled, "The Supplication of Beggars." The words of it were something in this style: "They complained of being defrauded of the alms usually given them, by the increasing number of idle vagabond friars, priests, monks, pardoners, and all the train in their employ, who visited every house, and compelled each person to contribute to their support under various pretexts. The writer calculated that they collected a sum which amounted to half the property and income of the nation, and thus rendered the people unable to bestow their accustomed charities." The vices and corruptions of priests and friars, and their desire to assume a power above the civil law, are therein forcibly dwelt upon. The writer also referred to the translation of the New Testament, and shewed that the clergy endeavoured to prevent the people from reading the Scriptures, because they clearly proved that their conduct was contrary to the Word of God; and set forth that remission of sins is not given by the Pope's pardon, but by Christ, for the sure faith and trust we have in him. The old chronicles of England relate many circumstances which unquestionably show that scenes of want and suffering, far more appalling than any of recent occurrence, were continually exhibited in the ages when Popery ruled our land.

During the time that Cromwel held the supreme command in ecclesiastical affairs, with the title of Vicar-General, a body of injunctions was issued under the sanction of the King and many of the bishops, by which several Romish superstitions were forbidden. These things, joined to the suppression of the lesser monasteries, which was being steadily carried on, occasioned much discontent amongst the bigoted Romanists, and many districts under their influence were led into open rebellion. While this raged, nothing appeared more plainly than the rooted enmity of the monastic orders to the appearance of any religious reformation: and it becoming evident, that nothing would reconcile those conventual bodies to their country's emancipation from Italian bondage, so long as abbeys and monasteries should be permitted to rear their heads over the whole country, a general suppression of them was thought expedient: and, as a preparative thereto, a new visitation of them was ordered, and the consequent exposure of monkish depravity, folly, &c., &c.,—which it is not purposed to detail in these pages,—naturally produced such disgust, that these societies all came forward of their own accord, as it was professed, and surrendered their houses to the Commissioners appointed by the Crown for that purpose.

On leaving their cloisters, the monks were provided with pensions and a sum of money as an outfit, proportioned to their respective conditions and good conduct. Some of the richer abbots received very handsome provisions, and indeed all the religious communities were treated equitably, if not liberally. This fact will partly explain why their suppression proved but moderately effective in replenishing the national purse. An immense mass of property was, indeed, surrendered into the King's hands, but it was heavily encumbered; and before the charges on it had worn out, it had chiefly passed, by means of grants and sales, from the sovereign to various private individuals. Six of the dissolved abbeys—Westminster, Oxford, Bristol, Gloucester, Chester, and Peterborough—were erected into bishops' sees, all of which yet remain, excepting Westminster, where the bishopric was discontinued after the death of its first prelate. Another judicious appropriation of conventual wealth was the foundation of Trinity College, Cambridge. From the suppressed monasteries, also, funds were supplied for completing the magnificent chapel of King's College in the same University. Towards the close of his life, Henry devoted to public uses more property, once monastic, founding Christ's and St. Bartholomew's Hospitals in London. Had all his appropriations of the wealth derived from convents resembled these, few persons would have questioned the propriety of placing this noble accumulation at his disposal.

Before we quit the subject of monasteries, we may make some remarks respecting the destruction of their libraries, and the probable loss thereby sustained of many valuable writings of ancient authors. This is a frequent charge, brought by those who are disposed to undervalue or lament the Reformation, against the suppression of monasteries; but, like many other of their charges, it is almost if not entirely groundless; for, on New-year's-day, 1545, Leland presented to the King a Report of his proceedings, under a Commission, which directed him to examine the libraries, and monasteries, and colleges which had been dissolved, that he might collect manuscripts relative to English history. Leland was well qualified for such an employment, and visited all parts of the kingdom on this errand. He stated that he had preserved many important works, and "that many things had come to light concerning the usurped authority of the Bishop of Rome and his accomplices." Leland also says that many of the authors he had preserved had already been printed in Germany and Italy. As to *British histories*, the chief destruction of them had been made some years *before*, by Polydore Virgil, an Italian by birth, but appointed Archdeacon of Wells, who wrote a History of England favourable to Romanism, and is reported to have destroyed all the copies of older authors which he could get into his possession, after he had availed himself of their contents. Doubtless this was to prevent his falsification of history being discovered. Moreover, there is sufficient evidence to satisfy any candid inquirer, that these libraries chiefly contained Romish books of devotion, legendaries, or tales of saints, missals, and other superstitious works, enough of which have been preserved to satisfy the most eager desire for such information; and the destruction of the remainder cannot be matter of just regret. These monasteries had, for the most part, been reared and populated during the dark ages, when literature and science were little cultivated; and the monks therein, exhibiting a far different character to those of earlier date, would, of course, then employ themselves in transcribing the works they most valued. It is also a well-attested fact, that from the scarcity and expense of parchment the monastic scribes of the *latter* ages were accustomed to erase the writings from such ancient manuscripts as were, by themselves, least esteemed, in order to transcribe homilies and extracts from the fathers, or legendary tales of the saints, in their stead. This practice had been carried to such an extent, that it is well known valuable manuscript portions of the Scriptures and many ancient writings were thus destroyed and written over.

But to return to the general subject: we must now state, that the steady proceedings of Henry in suppressing the monasteries, together with his countenancing the translation of the Scriptures, and rejection of the Pope's supremacy, brought to a crisis the indignation of the Pontiff, which had so long hung over him; for he now summoned Henry to appear before him, or forfeit his crown.* Henry's *subjects* also were instigated *to rebellion;* yet the monarch shrunk not beneath the

* The denunciations against Henry extended also to such of his subjects as did not oppose him to the utmost; and the bull contained the famous *Non obstante* clause, usual in the Pope's bulls, which declares that whatever the Pope decreed should take place, notwithstanding any constitutions or ordinances of the apostles which might be contrary to his decrees; thus setting up the words of the Pope as superior to the Word of God. The bull concludes by declaring, that if any persons should attempt to oppose this decree, they would incur the indignation of the Omnipotent God, and St. Peter and St. Paul, his apostles. Thus the reader may perceive that belief in the infallibility of the Pope necessarily includes a belief that he has the power to depose all sovereigns who offend him.

Pope's frown or his fulminated vengeance; for, after his mind appears to have been made up on the matter, he never ceased to maintain that God's undoubted Word is the only source of religious knowledge. Under the King's sanction, therefore, the Bible was translated into English, and was allowed to circulate freely throughout the country. In A.D. 1540, a new edition was issued and sent forth, every parish being bound under a heavy fine to provide a copy; and thus the Scriptures were dispersed throughout the whole kingdom. The manner in which the sacred volume was universally received, and the careful attention paid it, alarmed the Romanists; for its ruinous operations on their principles they well knew. Their policy, therefore, was to surrender, without a struggle, every question more immediately concerning the Pope; and thus they were enabled to keep well with their Royal master, and by having possession of his ear, to prevent his thoroughly adopting the reforming views of Cranmer and Cromwel. Accordingly, their resistance was shrewdly dormant respecting the Pontiff's supremacy, while they never yielded or gained a political point, but they endeavoured to obtain some restriction being placed on the Bible; and thus, after much exertion, the Romanist party at last prevailed on the King to withhold it from the humbler classes of society. This soon led to a fuller triumph—even the passing of the Act of the Six Articles. Cranmer offered a strenuous resistance to this iniquitous measure, and although warned by Henry to leave the House of Lords when he appeared to support it by his presence, he refused to do so, and opposed the Bill to the last. Cranmer manifested a bold and fearless conduct on this occasion, which is only one among many instances of the faithful manner in which he adhered to the truth, as far as he, at the time being, was enabled to perceive it. His views on religion were not so clear and distinct when he first appeared in public life as in later years, and this circumstance has been distorted to his disadvantage, although Mary consigned him to the flames as a heretic.

The leading provisions of this celebrated Act of the Six Articles were the following:—That the denial of transubstantiation should be punishable by burning; that attacks upon communion in one kind, upon the celibacy of the clergy, upon vows of chastity, upon private masses, or upon auricular confession, should render men liable to be hanged as felons. This barbarous Act was no sooner passed than the King's Romish advisers exerted themselves to have it carried into effect; but the victims taken up on its authority numbered so many that it happily embarrassed them; as putting so many as 500 to death at once might have caused a national outbreak; and, therefore, these supposed criminals were pardoned. The Romish party, however, attributing the failure very much to the influence of Cromwel, who had recently been created Earl of Essex, and was the acknowledged favourer of the Lollards, or Gospellers, (as they were then also called,) upon some false pretext excited the King's displeasure against him; who steeled his heart against Cranmer's and every other supplication that was made in behalf of his once valued and highly meritorious minister. Cromwel not being tried in open court, but attainted in Parliament as a heretic and traitor, was speedily led to the scaffold, where he met his end with the firmness becoming a Christian. Encouraged by his death, active measures were then commenced against the Lollards and reforming party. Numbers suffered as heretics,* and the Romanists succeeded in obtaining a prohibition against the free use of the Scriptures; and the subtlety of Gardiner, in further trying to render them unintelligible to the generality of readers, can only be accounted for by his being a Papist. After this prohibition against the Bible, no more versions of it were issued in Henry's time.†

With a view to supply the loss of the same, and to try and establish a uniformity of opinion, Henry published a book, called "The King's Book." This celebrated treatise began with a declaration of faith, the soundness or unsoundness of which is not necessary to be here canvassed. It then proceeded to an explanation of the Apostles' Creed, the Ten Commandments, and the Lord's Prayer. It cannot be considered as setting forth the doctrines of the Reformation, as secured to the Church of England by Henry's children and successors on the throne, Edward of blessed, and Elizabeth of glorious, memory; still it must be allowed that the doctrines of the Reformation appeared to have gained ground, though many Popish errors were asserted, and the restrictions on the general reading of the Bible not removed.‡ Henry's reign was now waning to its close; for he was advancing in years, and his increasing infirmities and consequent peevishness and irritability of temper, more than ever laid him open to the flatteries of his Romish courtiers, while the conscientious scruples of the Reforming party often excited his displeasure.

* See "Fox's Martyrs;" "History of the Lollards;" "Burnet's History of the Reformation."
† See Appendix, No. 3.
‡ As a proof of the high estimation in which the Holy Scriptures were held, it may be stated, that, about the year 1543, John Mar-

[A. D. 1542.] In this year, however, it was ordered in Convocation, that all books used in the Church should be examined; that superstitious prayers, legends, &c., &c., should be erased, and that one chapter of the New Testament should be read at morning and evening service. Moreover, occasional prayers, and in English, were introduced into the public service of the Church. Cranmer appears to have been the principal promoter of this important alteration; and, in the succeeding year, we again find him, as Archbishop, directing prayers to be made for a providential change of weather: and when the King, in A. D. 1544, was about to embark on an expedition against France, public prayers were ordered to be offered up for his success. The Royal mandate directed that these prayers were to be set forth to the people in the English tongue, that they, "feeling the godly taste thereof, may godlily and joyously, with thanks, receive, embrace, and frequent the same." Thus to Henry and Cranmer do we owe, not only the introduction of occasional prayers into public worship, but of its being also performed in a language intelligible to the mass of the congregation. These exertions of Cranmer in behalf of the purity of the Church services excited much enmity against him, and many persons suffering for the truth under the rigorous Act of Six Articles fearfully tell against the monarch and the Romish party.

beck, of Windsor, was taken up and examined on a charge of heresy for having begun an *English Corcordance* of the *Bible*, being the *first* that had been attempted in that language. He was condemned to the flames, but his life was spared. He was, however, doomed to perpetual imprisonment. Marbeck survived to the reign of Elizabeth, and from his testimony much information was obtained respecting the treatment and sufferings of the martyrs.

The latter now planned and endeavoured to carry forward many a scheme, not only against the Archbishop, but also against Catharine Parr, the last of Henry's queens: for her religious opinions, it was well known, were inclined to those of the Reformation; and being also possessed of a considerable share of good sense and information, she had become an ally of some importance to that cause.* The machinations of the Romish party against these two distinguished individuals were not permitted, by the providence of God, to prevail. The details of these intriguing plots need not be entered upon in this limited sketch of England's Church history, because they may be found explicitly set forth in most other works—even those of a mere secular character. For the same reason has the death of the martyrs, who, at prior dates, suffered as heretics, Lollards, or Gospellers, been scarcely more than referred to: so, again, shall now be passed over the dying testimonies of those who suffered as such at the close of Henry's reign. It is, indeed, a privilege to be able to escape from the task of describing scenes of such heart-rending and thrilling reality; or from the necessity of portraying the wasted forms of martyrs, sinking beneath the ravages of age, of sorrow, or of torture, as ever and anon they still advanced to the stake. No; we will not pause to record even their last prayer, nor to proclaim afresh the indignant murmurs wrung from the hearts of those who beheld their faith and their sufferings. It almost seemed that the fifth seal, mentioned in the Apocalypse, had been opened, and that these martyrs' cries had already reached the courts of heaven in the words therein recorded: (Rev. vi. 10.) "How long, O Lord, holy and

* Coverdale, the translator of the Bible, and afterwards Bishop of Exeter, was one of her chaplains. See Appendix, No. 3.

true, dost thou not judge and avenge our blood on them that dwell on the earth?" For now the monarch, who had so long permitted this sinful persecution to rage, and cut off such of his subjects as were "slain for the Word of God and the testimony which they held" against his still-favoured Romish creed, seemed to have so far wearied the long-suffering of the Lord, that the sentence was sent forth against himself: "Cut it down, why cumbereth it the ground?" for early on the morning of January 28, 1547, the last of England's Henrys closed his eyes in death.

No monarch's character has been, perhaps, so variously depicted as that of Henry VIII. It is scarcely necessary to say, that Romish writers describe him in the blackest colours. The Jesuits, Parsons and Sanders, were the principal authors of those glaring fabrications which falsify facts; and though they have been often refuted by the clearest evidence, yet their assertions have been, and are still, for some wily purpose, repeated, as if they had never been disproved. Probably, his having been raised up by the hand of God, as His kingly pioneer in politically clearing the way for the future establishment of the Reformation in these realms, was an offence in their sight quite sufficient to induce them to represent Henry—whatever he might have been—as a monster of iniquity. In now reviewing his character, let us bear in mind that he lived in a time distinguished by a very remarkable revolution in human affairs; and that the Lord's hand is not shortened, and, therefore, He works his purposes as seemeth him good; sometimes by the ablest, sometimes by the humblest, or by the holiest, or by the vilest of men; yet none may say unto Him, "What doest Thou?"

This is certain, that Henry was possessed of great

abilities, and had so early and highly cultivated them that as soon as he was called to the throne, he was prepared to enter upon theological disputes with pleasure and not reluctance. But having been educated according to the Romish creed and principles instead of the purifying precepts of the Gospel, we cannot wonder that all the evil propensities of his unregenerate heart were strengthened rather than diminished. The force, therefore, of early prejudices, aided by the unceasing watchfulness of an artful political party, blinded his strong understanding, and he was led into many acts of violence. This caused him to send to the scaffold those who opposed his regal authority, and to the stake those who differed from him as regarded the Romish creed: but happily for the future establishment of the Reformation, the same strength of mind and impetuosity of temper led him fearlessly onward in a course which, perhaps, a better regulated mind and heart would have hesitated to tread, but which enabled him to throw off the iron yoke of Popery. The safety and influence enjoyed and exercised by Gardiner, Bonner, and others who continued publicly to profess *only* the *religious doctrines* of the Church of Rome, prove that those alone suffered who advocated her political power and usurpations.

Numerous and heinous as Henry's religious, political, and social crimes may have been, it is certain, from the concurring testimony of historians, that he remained highly popular with his subjects to the last,— a convincing proof that the majority of the people did not regret the line of conduct he took with reference to the Church of Rome, and that in his general proceedings he acted in a manner less hateful than has commonly been represented. It is a satisfaction to state, that this monarch is also allowed to have been most attentive and anxious respecting the education of the Royal children, all of whom, with the exception of those who died in infancy, succeeded him on the throne. Henry's *latest* views also happily appear to have become more decided against the *doctrines* of Popery, and this is inferred from the circumstance, that the King of France and himself were in treaty together respecting the abolition of the mass, by changing it into a communion. Cranmer thus wrote to his secretary, Morice,—" If I should tell you what communication was had between the King's Highness and the French ambassador, (the King leaning upon him and me,) concerning the establishment of sincere religion, a man would hardly believe it; nor had I myself thought the King had been so forward in these matters as he then appeared." With all Henry's contradiction of character, much as Romanists may now desire to disown him, they cannot gainsay the fact of his having been educated in strict accordance with their Church's creed and discipline, and that he acted under its influence to the last; for he left his subjects writhing under the rigorous pressure of the Act of Six Articles, and, moreover, enriched that Church's coffers by ordering masses to be said for the repose of his soul. In summing up the actual effects that Henry VIII. produced while he swayed the sceptre of these realms, we must first observe, that, notwithstanding the guilt which attaches to his own personal conduct, he was the means, under the directing hand of the Most High, of greatly purifying the religious profession of his people. Having attacked Popery in its strongholds,—the monasteries, and destroyed them all, since tolerated they could not be, because they were proved to be the manufactories of Romish fraud, the nurseries of Romish superstition; and having flung off indignantly the Pope's supremacy, and the intolerable yoke by which the Roman bishops insulted the national independence and sapped the foundation of public morality, Henry cleared the way for all that came after—even to our days. Moreover, under his Royal authority, he caused the Creed, the Lord's Prayer, and the Ten Commandments to be taught to the people in English, and at length he ordered the Litany to be said in the same language. The most important, however, of his measures for enlightening his people was his authorizing an English version of the Bible. He did, indeed, afterwards attempt to restrict the use of the Sacred Volume; but streams of light had flowed from it over every portion of the land, and there was hence no danger of a speedy national return to the thick night of spiritual darkness which had recently prevailed. It is much to be lamented that a sovereign, who rendered so many important services to his country, should, in other matters, have brought upon his memory such a heavy load of just reproach, that it furnishes those who dislike or disapprove of the Reformation with a pretence for painting him in the most hateful colours; while such as rightly value the services he rendered to religion, have the pain of admitting that they were effected by a monarch whose memorable career was sullied by vice and tyranny.

Henry being consigned to the tomb, we find the proposed subject of these pages is brought to its close; for when his son, Edward VI., ascended the throne, the vitality of Christian principles was so engrafted in his heart, that under the sway of his sceptre, the Reformation was speedily brought about and the Protestant faith nationally established. And truly it yet shines as the brightest and only imperishable jewel that has adorned the brows of any of Britain's monarchs since the pristine days of Lucius.*

The writer has now, therefore, to request the young reader not to cast aside the subject which has been under consideration, but to turn to the pages of those established and trustworthy authors as not only base their evidences of Church and religious matters on that of Protestant testimony; but who, being themselves free from Romish, or Latitudinarian principles or prejudices, verify its onward progress under their safe guidance through the brief reign of Edward, and the Protestant reign of terror in that of Mary, and further, read in that of Elizabeth of the final establishment and triumph of the Reformation. Then let each one rejoice at the blessings which the perseverance, stedfastness, sufferings, and death of so many of our forefathers have secured to us by that happy event; but, whilst rejoicing, let all meditate on the responsibilities thereby entailed on the present generation, not only as regards our own eternal welfare, but that perhaps of generations yet unborn.

Young reader, now reflect that the soul is of too much consequence for you to hazard its salvation on you know not what; and forget not, that the Lord, the Head of the Church, has called you not only outwardly to acknowledge him, but to believe and obey the Gospel.

And for the encouragement of those just entering on the trials which must beset a Christian's path in these conflicting days, remember that whatever difficulties attend you in your heavenward course, your refuge and strength is near, and that believing prayer availeth much with Him, whose everlasting arm made and guides the

* See page 69.

universe. Further—ask of God,—Lord, what wilt thou have me to do? And whatsoever God shows you is your work of duty, do it while it is called to-day: put on the whole armour of God, (Eph. vi. 11—18,) and then, as Christ's faithful servants and soldiers, do it fearlessly as Protestants, both for England and for Ireland.

And now, Reader,—Farewell.

APPENDIX.

No. I.

GENERAL OBSERVATIONS ON THE WORD PROTESTANT.

THE word Protestant is not an ill-chosen or insignificant one; it has a precise, *positive*, and most noble meaning. The familiar and technical use of the word in later times has altogether wrested the verb "*to protest*" from its proper meaning, and in common use it has acquired a relative signification. We are apt to suppose that there can be no *protestation* except there be something to protest against. This is the root of the error of which Romanists and others avail themselves, to represent it as a mere negative of Romish errors.

This interpretation of the word protest is altogether false. To begin at home. Johnson interprets the word, "To give a solemn declaration of opinion or resolution." According to Johnson, therefore, a Protestant is "one who gives a solemn declaration of opinion or resolution."

The French Academy interprets the verb "*protester*—assurer ou promettre *positivement*." A Protestant in France is, therefore, one who gives a "*positive* assurance or promise."

The Latin dictionaries all interpret the word *protestor* as, to "testify, bear witness." The meaning of the word *protestans*, therefore, in Latin, in which language it was first used as a religious title, is "a witness," "a witness for the truth;" and this meaning is

230   APPENDIX.

supported by Hesychius and all the later Greek lexicographers, who uniformly translate *protestor* by the word Διαμαρτύρομαι—" I am a witness."

This verbal discussion may seem uncalled for; but we are constrained to prove the ignorance or dishonesty of those who would frighten us from the use of our glorious name of "*Protestant*" by describing it as something "cold," "negative," &c. It is nothing of the kind; it is the most illustrious of titles, "a witness for the Divine truth"—a *martyr*, we should say, if that word had not been consecrated by later usage to those witnesses—how many of them Protestants!—who have sealed their testimony with their blood.

The question next arises, Were they who in the sixteenth century assumed the name of *witnesses for the Divine truth*, or Protestants, entitled to assume it? They were. They were the first who for nearly ten centuries had even sought to ascertain and define what the truth is. "The Church of Rome," says Basnage, "has never dared to make a confession of faith; because, changing its dogmas every instant, and never being sure of its principles, a detail of its doctrines would afford too good means for discovering its innovations." The "witnesses for the truth," the Protestants, had no such fear, and therefore their very first step was to extract, with care and reverence, from the holy Scriptures, a compendium of all the essential truths to which it was their purpose to testify. The formulary of Melancthon, drawn up in 1527, was one of the earliest of the attempts to form a compendium; it is divided into eighteen chapters, of which two or three at the most have any reference to Romanist corruptions, the rest all treating of the essential truths of religion, the same essential truths which we have handed down to us, with little change in the form of expression, in the Articles of our own Church.

This was more than two years before the Diet of Spires, at which the *witnesses* for the truth assumed the Latin name of witnesses,—Protestants. Here, then, was something positive—a clear, distinct, and definite confession of faith, embracing all the essential truths of Christianity given to the world, which previously had received no such confession for a thousand years, and had lost that which had been previously vouchsafed in an ocean of superstitions. It was *Romanism*, not *Protestantism*, that was the *negative*, and the distinction still continues the same. The term Protestantism may, therefore, be considered as expressive of *a complete confession of religious faith*, independent of the existence even of the Church of Rome, or of any other Church, and, therefore, not necessarily or essentially adverse to any Church, except as truth is always adverse to falsehood.

No. II.

GENERAL OBSERVATIONS ON LITURGIES.

THE Liturgy or collection of public prayers contained in the "Apostolic Constitutions"—the origin of which assumes a doubtful character—is the oldest composition of its kind now extant. It was, probably, composed about the beginning of the fourth century, or a little earlier; and although it does not appear to have been used in its present form by any Church, yet it seems to have been the basis upon which other Liturgies were successively constructed. The Liturgy is, therefore, highly interesting and important, on account of its great antiquity, and as being the model by which the public devotions of Churches were afterwards, in a great measure, regulated. There is no proof, however, of the existence of any of these ancient formularies earlier than the fifth century, with the exception of that of St. Basil, which is traced with some degree of certainty to the fourth.

Ancient British, or Gallican Liturgy.

Germanus is supposed to have introduced the use of the Gallican Liturgy into the British Church, which was derived from St. John, through Polycarp and Irenæus. The principal differences between this and the Roman Liturgy are stated to be followed in the Common Prayer-book of the Church of England; so that the Reformers, when they translated and made the selections from the services of the Church of Rome, really reduced back the form of prayers to a nearer conformity to our ancient Liturgy.

Anglo-Saxon Liturgy.

The Anglo-Saxon Liturgy was formed from the sacramentary of Gregory the Great, and by a comparison of our Book of Common Prayer with it, it is evident, that almost all the Collects for our Sundays and festivals were taken from his contemplations. As, however, each bishop had the power of making improvements in the Liturgy of his Church, in process of time different customs arose, and several became so established as to receive the names of "Uses or Customs" of York, Sarum, Hereford, Bangor, Lincoln, Aberdeen; and were thus distinguished from each other.

The Romish Missal, &c., Rites, and Ceremonies had the ascendancy during the dark ages in Britain.

(A.D. 1546.)

[A.D. 1546.] The King's Primer was printed by authority; the object thereof being to furnish the unlearned with such parts of the Church service as were most required, as well as to supply them with the Creed, the Lord's Prayer, and the Ten Commandments in the vulgar tongue.

[A.D. 1549.] The first Liturgy of Edward VI. appeared. This book forms a kind of connecting link between the Missal and the Prayer-book. The principle on which the compilers proceeded in the work was, to alter as little as possible what had been familiar to the people. One hundred and sixteen addresses to the apostles, the Virgin Mary, and different saints, were left out. In the Litany the following petition was inserted:—" That we may be delivered from the tyranny of the Pope." And the service was entirely performed in English.

[A.D. 1552.] When a few years had enabled the Christian community to examine the new Common Prayer-book, and some persons were hardly satisfied with it, it was determined to make a general review of the whole, under the direction of Cranmer, with the assistance of other divines—the same, probably, as had originally compiled it. The sentences, exhortation, confession, and absolution, with which the service now begins were introduced. In the Communion Service also the decalogue was added.

(A.D. 1560.)

[A.D. 1560.] On the re-establishment of Protestantism by Queen Elizabeth, one of her first cares was to review the Common Prayer-book; and, after due examination and consideration, the second of Edward was selected, and but few alterations were made therein.

Such is the general sketch of the Liturgies of the Church of England, which, on account of not breaking the connexion of the same, has been brought to a later date than the death of Henry VIII.

No. III.

BIBLES.

THE Britons possessed the Holy Scriptures in some abundance previous to the Diocletian persecution; but, in consequence of the great destruction of them, which took place whilst that raged in Britain after that period, they became very scarce.

The Anglo-Saxons possessed the Holy Scriptures in their native language. The first person who published the Bible in English was John Wickliff. His translation is made from the Vulgate, as he was unacquainted with the original languages. Notwithstanding the opposition which was raised against it when it made its appearance, and the efforts to prevent its distribution and to procure its destruction, numerous copies of it still remain. The difficulty of multiplying copies must have created a constant hinderance to the general use of the Scriptures, had not the overruling power of the Most High ordained that the art of printing should, as it were, open a way for the Reformation of the Church, and materially assist its progress.

[A.D. 1526.] The first person who printed any part of the Bible in English was William Tyndale. He was proceeding in this task in Flanders, whither he had been driven by the hand of persecution, when even in that foreign land he did not escape from it; for he was exalted to a better world through the trial of martyrdom —a crown, to which his associates in the work were afterwards called.

[A.D. 1535.] But the glory of putting forth the first Bible in print was reserved for Miles Coverdale, chaplain of Catherine Parr, last queen of Henry VIII. Coverdale afterwards became Bishop of Exeter.

[A. D. 1537.] In this year another edition appeared, which passes under the name of Matthew's, and is partly taken from Tyndale and partly from Coverdale. It was put forth under this fictitious name, probably by John Rogers, who wished to conceal himself through the fear of persecution. It was of this Bible that an impression of 2,500 copies was burnt at Paris, in 1538, by the Inquisition, though Francis I. had given leave for its being printed there. On the 4th of February, 1555, John Rogers, then Vicar of St. Sepulchre's, was the first martyr in the reign of Mary, being taken to Smithfield and there burnt: his wife and eleven children being denied an interview with him, they obtained a passing sight of each other as he went through the streets.

[A. D. 1539.] "The great Bible," under the superintendence of Cranmer and by the permission of Henry, has principally acquired the name of the Archbishop from the preface he wrote to the second edition. It is from this edition, with very slight variations, that the Psalms in the Prayer-book are taken.

[A. D. 1568.] When a new edition of the great Bible was required for the use of parish churches, in the reign of Queen Elizabeth, Archbishop Parker, being unwilling to put it forth again, without endeavouring to correct all the errors which had been observed in it, employed a number of learned divines to aid him in the task of making it as perfect as possible. As the majority of the persons employed were bishops, this edition of the Bible has been ordinarily denominated the Bishops' or Parker's Bible.

[A. D. 1604.] In consequence of certain objections raised against the Bishops' Bible in the conference which took place at Hampton Court, a new translation was agreed on. As little alteration as possible was to be made in it by the learned divines and scholars who were appointed to the important task, and who numbered forty-seven. No notes were to be affixed beyond what the literal explanation of the Hebrew and Greek words adopted into the text might require, and a few marginal references, and only a few, were to be appended. The persons appointed to the work entered on the execution of it in the spring of 1607; but the Bible was not printed till 1611, so much time and caution were used to prevent inaccuracies. This edition is that now in use in the Church of England.

APPENDIX. 235

No. IV.
CANONS.

CANON is a word not exclusively belonging to any particular Church, but may be applied to the ecclesiastical rules of any Church or religious community which that body may select for their own guidance or government.

As regards those which are now in operation in the Church of England they number 141, and form the basis of ecclesiastical law, as far as the clergy are concerned. As they were never ratified by Act of Parliament, though sanctioned by Royal assent at the Conference of Hampton Court in 1604, in law they are not held to bind the laity. Many of them have been superseded by Act of Parliament. *except in the practice of the Ecclesiastical in marriage. I will c*

No. V.
A FEW OBSERVATIONS ON THE PROGRESS OF THE REFORMATION IN IRELAND.

AFTER having read at page 204 that not a sword was drawn in Ireland in behalf of the Romish Hierarchy when Henry VIII. cast off the supremacy of the Pope, and announced himself the head of the Church, the reflecting reader may, perhaps, be glad to know why the happy effects of the Reformation did not ultimately progress there in the same ratio and with the same lasting benefit as in England. The unwise edict of Henry VIII., mentioned in page 208, which interfered in non-essential customs, such as dress, mode of cutting the hair and beard, &c., &c., and which long habit had made a second nature, were sufficient to induce a half-civilized and enthusiastic people to unsheath the sword of resistance against their rulers, and thus prepared the way for the political advances of designing men during the reigns of Edward and Mary. By a merciful interposition of God, the Protestants in Ireland were preserved during the reign of Mary; and when at last the time had arrived that she considered it was safe and desirable to send amongst them the scourge of persecution, in the form of a Commission for the punishment of heretics of Ireland, the fatal document was extracted from the dispatch-box, and a pack of cards, with the knave of clubs placed uppermost, was substituted in its stead. Before the artifice could be remedied by Mary, her days were numbered, and thus Christ's Church in Ireland escaped her wrath.

When Elizabeth mounted the throne, it is notorious in history that the Reformation had been generally received in Ireland by the nobles, priests, and people. The bishops (with the exception of two) and the priests of Rome all outwardly conformed, substituting the Prayer-book for the Missal, and the English Service for the Latin Mass. They could then discover no heresy in our book of prayer, or anything damnable in our public service, but a new light flashed upon them from Rome in the Order of Jesuits; and amidst the members of that extraordinary fraternity, (which is in force even in these later days,) many a master mind and accomplished political intriguant was then, as may still, be found. "The most exquisite and refined subtlety, the most brilliant and attractive talents, the most accomplished spirit of intrigue and diplomacy, combined with all the power that religious genius and wealth could confer, were the attributes with which the order of Jesuits, in Elizabeth's time, flung itself, with all the passion of a desperate fidelity, into the service of the Church of Rome. They were found in the palace and in the hovel, in the camp and in the hall, leading the song of revel to-night, and joining in the hymn of the choir to-morrow, till there was no place and no circumstance in which they had not a share." Such was the description given of Jesuits in Elizabeth's days, and they remain unchanged in principle and in practice in our own. It was, however, from this fraternity that the Court of Rome selected its agents, who were to accomplish the work of checking the Reformation in both England and Ireland. While Campion and Parsons were sent to the former, Saunders and Allen were sent to the latter; and, in strict accordance with their established rule, their operations were to be regulated by the circumstances of each country. The Pope resolved to depose Elizabeth, and, therefore, the Jesuits traversed the land and proclaimed that she was excommunicated; that all her ordinances, whether civil or ecclesiastical, were invalid; and produced what, in those dark times, was deemed equally authoritative with the law of God, the Papal Bull for the formal excommunication and deposition of the Queen. Hatred to England as an invader, and hatred to Protestantism as a heresy, was fanned into a rebel blaze by his agents, which spread like wildfire through the length and breadth of the land. The Desmonds and Geraldines were in arms, the cry of battle was heard in all the deep recesses of Ireland, and the clans were gathered under their respective chiefs, while *the plenary remission of their sins* was granted to all who joined the rebel standard. But candour obliges it to be acknowledged that all these efforts, aided and supported by every artifice which could be devised or resorted to, would have fallen powerless before the force of truth and the armour of righteousness, had not the wretched policy of England fatally combined with the plans of her enemies to arrest the progress of the Reformation. As if the hateful and impolitic statutes of Kilkenny, and of Henry VIII., were not sufficient to disaffect the national feeling and subvert the Protestant cause in Ireland, a statute was again enacted in the second of Elizabeth, by which it was made lawful to say or use all their common and open prayers in the Latin tongue. Thus, every avenue of light and knowledge, under the withering statute-book of England, was at once closed upon the Irish by their being deprived of instruction in their own language,—that in which only an illiterate people can think; and either the hateful English, or the equally unintelligible Latin, was substituted in its place. Can we suppose anything less than judicial blindness to have prompted measures calculated at once to exasperate prejudice, and involve in midnight darkness, a people wedded to their own customs, and fond to excess of their own language, and already stung to the quick at the dishonour cast on their national dress? One generation of professing, but, alas! uninstructed Protestants, passed away, succeeded by another, brought up, if possible, in a state of greater ignorance, and thus have they continued to disappear from off the face of the earth for three centuries. Can we wonder at the effects produced?—effects which England too justly feels the bitterness of, even at the present day!

N.B.—Any reader who may feel interested in the further fate of Ireland is urged to well study Dean Murray's "Ireland and her

Church." And such as are especially desirous to assist the Protestant cause there, in connexion with the United Church of England and Ireland, are referred to a pamphlet written by J. E. Gordon, Esq., entitled, " The Church of Ireland considered in her Ecclesiastical relation to the Roman Catholic part of the Population;" and are urged to direct their attention also to the Reports and efforts of those Societies especially established to meet the spiritual exigencies of the Irish at the present time.

MACINTOSH, PRINTER,
GREAT NEW STREET, LONDON.

Works published by

WERTHEIM AND MACINTOSH,

24, PATERNOSTER-ROW, LONDON.

In foolscap 8vo., with ornamental title-page, cloth lettered, 5s. 6d.,
The PILGRIM'S HAND-BOOK: or, Counsel and Comfort for the Wayfarers of Zion. Set forth by a PILGRIM.
"Plain directions, wise counsels, and sure comforts."

ALSO,

GOOD OUT of EVIL: or, the History of Adjai, an African Slave-boy. By a Lady. With an Introductory Notice by the Rev. C. F. CHILDE, M.A., Principal of the Church Missionary College, and Evening Lecturer of St. Mary's, Islington. Price 3s. 6d.

SERMONS and OUTLINES of SERMONS. By the late J. D. LANE, M.A., Rector of Forncett St. Peter's, and formerly Fellow of St. John's College, Cambridge. Cloth, 6s.

ANATOMICO-THEOLOGY; or, a Critical Dissertation of various Scriptures, explanatory of the Doctrines, Precepts, Hopes, and Prospects of the Christian Religion. By the Rev. THOMAS BAGNALL-BAKER, M.A. 8vo., cloth, 10s. 6d.

PLAIN SERMONS. By the Rev. EDWARD CROW, M.A., Incumbent of Tuckingmill, Cornwall. Second Edition. Cloth, 3s. 6d.

FAITH and PRACTICE. Sermons by the Rev. S. GOMPERTZ, Minister of Chalford Episcopal Chapel, Gloucestershire. 4s.

SERMONS on some of the LEVITICAL TYPES. By HORATIO JAMES, M.A., Vicar of Coln St. Aldwyn's, Gloucestershire. Cloth, 4s. 6d.

An EXPOSITION upon the two EPISTLES of the Apostle St. PAUL to the THESSALONIANS. By the Rev. Father in God JOHN JEWELL, Bishop of Salisbury. A New Edition, carefully revised and corrected. Cloth, 3s. 6d.

LECTURES on Subjects connected with the SECOND ADVENT of our LORD and SAVIOUR. Preached during Lent, by CLERGYMEN OF THE CHURCH OF ENGLAND. Cloth, 3s. 6d.

PLAIN SERMONS on Subjects Practical and Prophetic. By Rev. A. M'CAUL, D.D., Prebendary of St. Paul's, and Rector of St. James's, Dukeplace. Cloth, 6s. 6d.

BARRACK SERMONS, preached in the Cavalry Barracks at Dorchester. By Rev. HENRY MOULE, Vicar of Fordington, Dorset. 2s. 6d.

WORKS PUBLISHED BY WERTHEIM AND MACINTOSH.

SCRIPTURAL CHURCH TEACHING. By the same Author. The Doctrinal, Experimental, and Practical Teaching of the Church of England, and the Encouragement and Direction given to Scriptural and Faithful Prayer, in the Selection of the Epistle and Gospel, and First Lessons, and in the Collect for the Sundays and chief Festivals in the course of the Year. Cloth, 2s. 6d.

The CHURCH of ENGLAND, APOSTOLICAL in its ORIGIN, EPISCOPAL in its GOVERNMENT, and SCRIPTURAL in its BELIEF; wherein, also, its Claims in opposition to Popery and Dissent are considered and asserted. By Rev. THOMAS P. PANTIN, M.A., Westcote, Gloucestershire. 6d.

A BRIEF MEMOIR of the Rev. CHARLES SIMEON, M.A., late Vicar of Trinity Church, and Fellow of King's College, Cambridge. Cloth, 1s. 6d.

JUSTIFICATION by FAITH, cleared from Error, founded on Scripture, and built on the Testimony of Protestant Divines. By the Rev. JAMES G. FAITHFULL, M.A., Vicar of North Mimms, Herts. Cloth, 4s. 6d.

JOURNAL of MISSIONARY LABOURS in JERUSALEM. By the Rev. F. C. EWALD. Second Edition. Cloth, 4s. 6d.

EMILY BATHURST; or, at Home and Abroad. By the Author of "Book for Young Women." Cloth, 3s.

The AUTOBIOGRAPHY of MAUDE BOLINGBROKE. A Roman Catholic Story. By EMMA JANE, Author of "Alice Cuninghame," &c. Cloth, 5s.

The COUNTRY and LONDON. A Tale for Children. By the Author of "Aids to Development," &c., &c. With Engravings. Cloth, 2s.

ANNA, the LEECH VENDOR. A Narrative of Filial Love. Third Edition. Cloth, 1s.

"This is as pretty a tale as we can well meet with."—*Christian Lady's Mag.*

The CHRISTIAN LYRE: A Selection of Religious and Moral Poetry. Cloth, 1s. 6d.; morocco, 3s. 6d.

EARLY TRAINING; or, Warnings and Encouragements for Christian Parents. Cloth, 1s.

A MANUAL of Short PRAYERS for Private Devotion. By the Rev. ABNER W. BROWN, M.A., Author of "Memoir of Abner and David Brown." "Hymns and Chants for Children of the Church of England," &c., &c. 6d., or in cloth, 1s.

The CHURCH MILITANT and TRIUMPHANT; or, an Arrangement of Texts of Scripture on the Subject. By the WIFE OF A CLERGYMAN. Second Edition. Price 1s.

Catalogues of Wertheim and Macintosh's Publications can be obtained.

Trieste Publishing has a massive catalogue of classic book titles. Our aim is to provide readers with the highest quality reproductions of fiction and non-fiction literature that has stood the test of time. The many thousands of books in our collection have been sourced from libraries and private collections around the world.

The titles that Trieste Publishing has chosen to be part of the collection have been scanned to simulate the original. Our readers see the books the same way that their first readers did decades or a hundred or more years ago. Books from that period are often spoiled by imperfections that did not exist in the original. Imperfections could be in the form of blurred text, photographs, or missing pages. It is highly unlikely that this would occur with one of our books. Our extensive quality control ensures that the readers of Trieste Publishing's books will be delighted with their purchase. Our staff has thoroughly reviewed every page of all the books in the collection, repairing, or if necessary, rejecting titles that are not of the highest quality. This process ensures that the reader of one of Trieste Publishing's titles receives a volume that faithfully reproduces the original, and to the maximum degree possible, gives them the experience of owning the original work.

We pride ourselves on not only creating a pathway to an extensive reservoir of books of the finest quality, but also providing value to every one of our readers. Generally, Trieste books are purchased singly - on demand, however they may also be purchased in bulk. Readers interested in bulk purchases are invited to contact us directly to enquire about our tailored bulk rates. Email: customerservice@triestepublishing.com

You May Also Like

The Lost Found, and the Wanderer Welcomed

W. M. Taylor

ISBN: 9780649639663
Paperback: 188 pages
Dimensions: 6.14 x 0.40 x 9.21 inches
Language: eng

Reports of the Board of Directors and of the Superintendents of the State Hospitals for the Insane at Raleigh, Goldsboro and Morganton, North Carolina

State Hospital of North Carolina

ISBN: 9780649690602
Paperback: 114 pages
Dimensions: 6.14 x 0.24 x 9.21 inches
Language: eng

www.triestepublishing.com

You May Also Like

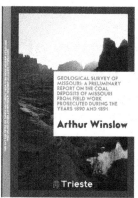

Geological Survey of Missouri: A Preliminary Report on the Coal Deposits of Missouri from Field Work Prosecuted During the Years 1890 and 1891

Arthur Winslow

ISBN: 9780649691807
Paperback: 244 pages
Dimensions: 6.14 x 0.51 x 9.21 inches
Language: eng

The University of Minnesota. The Calendar for the Year 1883-84

University Minneapolis

ISBN: 9780649057054
Paperback: 140 pages
Dimensions: 6.14 x 0.30 x 9.21 inches
Language: eng

www.triestepublishing.com

You May Also Like

1807-1907 The One Hundredth Anniversary of the incorporation of the Town of Arlington Massachusetts

Various

ISBN: 9780649420544
Paperback: 108 pages
Dimensions: 6.14 x 0.22 x 9.21 inches
Language: eng

Biennial report of the Board of State Harbor Commissioners, for the two fiscal years commencing July 1, 1890, and ending June 30, 1892

Various

ISBN: 9780649194292
Paperback: 44 pages
Dimensions: 6.14 x 0.09 x 9.21 inches
Language: eng

www.triestepublishing.com

You May Also Like

Biennial report of the Board of State Harbor Commissioners for the two fisca years. Commeneing July 1, 1884, and Ending June 30, 1886

Various

ISBN: 9780649199693
Paperback: 48 pages
Dimensions: 6.14 x 0.10 x 9.21 inches
Language: eng

Biennial report of the Board of state commissioners, for the two fiscal years, commencing July 1, 1890, and ending June 30, 1892

Various

ISBN: 9780649196395
Paperback: 44 pages
Dimensions: 6.14 x 0.09 x 9.21 inches
Language: eng

Find more of our titles on our website. We have a selection of thousands of titles that will interest you. Please visit

www.triestepublishing.com

Lightning Source UK Ltd.
Milton Keynes UK
UKOW01f1522231017
311488UK00008B/2249/P